MW00468793

TRUE
WORTH

IDENTITY IN CHRIST

MICHAEL J. LEWIS

True Worth
Published by True Worth Media
www.trueworthmedia.com

All rights reserved. No part of this publication may be reproduced, stored in a retrieval system, or transmitted in any form or by any means-electronic, mechanical, photocopy, recording, scanning, or other-except for brief quotations in critical reviews or articles, without the prior written permission of the publisher.

Published in the United States of America

Cover and Interior Design by Janelle Evangelides
Author photos by Tiffany Treadwell at Infinite Photography
Edited by Pat Stainke and Tom Catanzaro

All Scripture quotations, unless otherwise indicated, are taken from The Holy Bible, New International Version®. NIV®. Copyright © 1973, 1978, 1984, 2011.. Used by permission. All rights reserved. Italicized and bold emphasis in Scripture quotations are added by the author. Scripture quotations labeled NLT are taken from the Holy Bible, New Living Translation. © 1996, 2004, 2007, 2013.. Used by permission. All rights reserved. Italicized and bold emphasis in Scripture quotations are added by the author. Scripture quotations labeled ESV are taken from the Holy Bible, English Standard Version®. ESV®. Copyright © 2001.. Used by permission. All rights reserved. Italicized and bold emphasis in Scripture quotations are added by the author. Scripture quotations marked NKJV are taken from the New King James Version®. Copyright © 1982 by .. Used by permission. All rights reserved. Italicized and bold emphasis in Scripture quotations are added by the author.

ISBN .. 978-1-7358005-0-9 (Paperback)
ISBN .. 978-1-7358005-1-6 (eBook)
© 2020 Michael J. Lewis

For a FREE chapter-by-chapter worksheet, visit
www.trueworthmedia.com/true-worth-worksheet
For a FREE Bible study following along with
this book and for other studies, visit
www.trueworthmedia.com/bible-studies
For a FREE audiobook first chapter of
True Worth: Identity in Christ visit
www.trueworthmedia.com/true-worth-free-audio

Michael is a gifted story-teller. As you read through the pages of his book, you will be captivated with his passion to unravel the truth that sets readers free. He uncovers topics on who we are that are not commonly discussed and he provides practical ways to overcome our daily struggles. True Worth is an excellent read!

Claire Lewis – *A beautiful daughter of God created in His image*

I am truly humbled to witness the personal transformation of Michael and his lovely wife Claire. The impact of this offering will allow you to clearly perceive your identity in Christ in a world that bases your identity on facts, like that little ID card inside your wallet. God gave Michael these tools strategically to help you become more like Jesus Christ. As a skilled builder, he's laid the foundation through this powerful treasury you're about to read.

Allen Thomas Musaraca – *A man anointed by God to speak to nations*

Major perspective shifts! This book brings major clarity to the reason why we make the choices we do... our identity! Let's cut to the chase, if you want your life to remain the same, it's simple... put this book down because you can't read it and remain unchanged!

Jonathan Drouault – *God's beloved son who is worthy of every blessing and gift from Heaven*

Michael J. Lewis shows us how to shed false identities and titles we or others place upon ourselves. He shines light on the fact that only our identity in Christ truly matters. Empowering read!

Sara Adamchak – *More than a conqueror in Christ who listens when God speaks to her*

Michael Lewis is one of the most genuine people I know. His transparency and high moral character shine through this book in a way that both carries me toward the heart of the Father and challenges me to live in uncompromising faithfulness to Him. This book has set me free to be much more vulnerable with God and others.

Tom Catanzaro – *A royal priest who shows others the goodness of God*

True Worth is a game changer that really makes you think about who you are, an absolute must read.

Richard Garcia – *An ambassador for Christ telling the world, "Come back to God!"*

If you do not like the label on your "can," then read Michael's book True Worth! When we accept Christ in our hearts, all things are made new and we get a new label on our can of identity. Read the book to find out how your label is under attack, but you can fight back by changing each can you identify with!

Joshua Shugg – *A man worthy of Christ's death on the cross*

Michael takes a complex idea and turns it beautifully simple. Readers do not need any former understanding of psychology to get the message he is speaking of. Your identity in Christ needs to be greater than... fill in the blank. Definitely a book to read more than once. True Worth is applicable to all our different seasons of life!

Megan Yost – *A mighty warrior for Christ wielding a sword of light*

Michael Lewis provides an open and honest outlook that shines through his own various identities. He has opened himself up and the experiences he has faced to spread the message God has put into place for him. True Worth helps to remind myself of how I can be a better person and follow the plan that God has for me. I recommend this book to refresh yourself and your life and what God has in store for each of us.

David Fair – *A man who knows the truth which was imparted by the Spirit*

Michael Lewis brings to light the importance of "true worth" that lies in each one of us. Through humility and admissions of struggles, he uses biblical truths to bring understanding to the reader the freedom found in this simple truth.

Lori Reese Thrasher – *A woman anointed to lead the world to Christ*

What is our purpose in life and what's it worth? If you've ever wondered something similar, you will find True Worth: Identity in Christ by Michael Lewis a refreshing perspective for finding worth in Christ.

Jill Flynt –*A daughter of the Most High God entrusted to instruct the children of God*

People may go the rest of their lives without reaching their full potential, Michael does a great job while being truly genuine to help the reader see their full potential in the book, True Worth. Using scripture to help us see who we are, not according to the world, but to the one that matters, God.

Constance Bestwick – *A daughter appointed for a specific purpose from God*

Britt,

Thanks for the support. Looking forward to getting connected more and more through the years.

God bless

Michael Lewis

Special thanks.

To God for trusting me with this message.

To Claire, my beautiful wife and best friend, for supporting me through the process and believing in me.

CONTENTS

INTRODUCTION

KNOW ALSO THAT WISDOM IS LIKE HONEY FOR YOU: IF YOU FIND IT, THERE IS A
FUTURE HOPE FOR YOU, AND YOUR HOPE WILL NOT BE CUT OFF.
PROVERBS 24:14

YOU NEED TO HEAR THIS!

God cares about YOU. God has plans for YOUR life. God values YOU just as much as He values your pastor, your boss, the CEO of a huge company, and the homeless man on the street corner.

So why do we keep chasing higher titles, achievements, and statistics?

If we are to live the life of freedom promised by God, we must reject the bondage the world tries to place on us with the pursuit of artificial value.

Insecurity.

Frustration.

Pain.

Low self-esteem.

These are often the results of following the world's advice on how to live a successful and happy life. But why are so many Christians falling into these same patterns of worldly pursuits? The answer is simple: they have accepted Jesus' gift on the cross to save them, but they have not accepted the implications of their value derived from that gift.

Understanding that your true worth and value come from identity in Christ will change your daily interactions, your decisions, and the way you see other people. 1 Corinthians 7:23 says you were bought at a price – and that price was very high! His sacrifice on the cross is where your true worth is established.

Worldly pursuits. That phrase probably sounds icky to your Christian ears. We've been conditioned to express our distaste for these things while living in a world where they are a necessity. This is why many Christian teachings leave us feeling hypocritical, frustrated, and insecure. We know we're not supposed to find our value in earning money, but we still have to provide for our families. Therefore, we decide we cannot live the life God wants us to live because we have bills to pay.

You must make a distinction. There's a difference between pursuing those things and allowing them to determine your worth. I'm here to tell you, those worldly pursuits are not mutually exclusive to living the life Christ wants you to live here on Earth.

Is this book against the pursuit of prestigious titles, higher education, more money, and worldly achievements? Absolutely not! This book is making the case that your value does not come from those things. Identity in Christ is the awareness that your value is identical to everyone else's. When you know your true worth, you experience the freedom to pursue those worldly accomplishments without finding your value in them.

Throughout our daily walk, we act in a cycle of decisions and behaviors. Those decisions and behaviors are often a direct result of our identity.

This process of decisions and behaviors, when tied to our identity, usually follows the following cycle:

Proclaim – Project – Protect.

You proclaim who you are (identity). For example, "I am a nice person."

You then project who you are by doing – and show-ing yourself to be doing – nice things. (This often turns into doing things that others think make you a nice person.)

Then you protect that identity. When someone confronts you about doing something that "isn't nice," you will protect your nice image either by defending or retracting.

Understanding this cycle will advance your under-standing of why you do certain things you don't want to do. Furthermore, it will also give clarity as to why others do things you don't understand.

This book is designed to take you on a journey of understanding and clarity. Finding identity in Christ and the knowledge of your true worth brings freedom from judgment, condemnation, and insecurity. That paradigm shift will allow you to act each day within the scope of who you are truly meant to be with full knowledge of your true value.

The price Jesus paid for you on the cross is the high-est price possible, so you are worth so much more than any worldly accomplishment can express.

Understanding the value you have in Christ is vital to living a healthy Christian life.

My prayer is that you will read these pages and dis-cern the meaning and application to your life. Prayer-fully consider the message and implications and make adjustments to your life where the Holy Spirit leads.

Enjoy the journey!

1

WHAT IS IDENTITY

SET YOUR MINDS ON THINGS ABOVE, NOT ON EARTHLY THINGS.
COLOSSIANS 3:2

Identity. This word is tossed around in conversations, politics, and churches. The word itself can be used in different applications and assume different connotations, so I'd like to begin by clarifying how I use this term. For the purposes of this book, identity refers to the distinguishing characteristics, roles, and traits you ascribe to yourself. In other words, identity defines who you are. These aspects of your identity take several forms: job titles and descriptions, family status, positions you hold, locations, and many more.

Are there areas of your life that baffle you? Disappoint you? Do you ever wonder why you do some of the things you do? Do you want to see a change in your response to certain things?

In this book, we will go on a journey to discover the various identities we have that form our mindset and control our emotions, our actions, and our decisions. However, let me be clear about something: this is not a personality test. I'll leave that up to the psychologists of the world. As humans, we all relate to more than one identity; usually, various identities will vie to take precedence depending on our current location, situation, and people surrounding us. Follow me as I present this idea throughout the next few chapters of the book.

This is more than an attempt to discover the various identities in your personal makeup; it is a look inside to discover how each one controls your decisions. When you have a strong understanding of who you are and recognize the identities that operate within you, you will be able to use this information to make the changes you want to see in your life. Each identity automatically fits in a hierarchy according to the priorities we set for ourselves. This hierarchy is often determined subconsciously. However, a better awareness of how the hierarchy of identities is structured and consciously taking control of the structure can bring much more peace to your life.

In this book, I want you to become more aware of each of your identities. From there, I will give you the tools to become intentional about choosing how each one fits in your personal hierarchy based on your situation and need. Because when the hierarchy has been properly prioritized, you will make better decisions, lay a stronger foundation for your life, and succeed in those areas that are most important to you.

Did you ever wonder why some people do certain things that don't make a whole lot of sense to you? You may even see them do something repeatedly and wonder why they continue in the same behavior, especially if it doesn't seem to be working for them. No matter how well you know that person, you may not be able to discern the underlying identity that controls them in that situation. It might be based on how they believe others view them, how they view themselves, or something ingrained in them from long ago. Unless you can see that person's perception of who he is, you won't understand why he does things that seem peculiar to you.

Let's take a look in the mirror. Do you do things or make decisions and later wonder why you made those decisions? On the surface, your actions are probably influenced by three main factors: 1) how you believe others see you, 2) how you see yourself, and 3) the image you choose to present to others and the pressure you put on yourself to live up to that image.

We all live with the notion that others have expectations of us. To a great extent, this is normal and healthy. From childhood, we know what our parents expect of us. An important part of growing up in a healthy family or doing well in school is learning to conform to the expectations our parents, teachers, and neighbors have of us. However, once we reach an age of independence, it can be unhealthy to attach too much importance to other's expectations. Those expectations can become where we find our value if they are overemphasized.

With this in mind, ask yourself: have other people around you influenced your thinking because of certain expectations they had of you? How can this be? Whether consciously or subconsciously, are you allowing their expectations to control your actions and decisions?

On the other hand, do you feel a need to live up to your own personal identity? Is this something you have ascribed to yourself with your own words? Does it tie in with an image you are choosing to present to others in your world? You may have said something in the past about who you are.

Often, when we proclaim an identity, that leads us to project it to others through actions. Furthermore, we will feel the need to protect that identity when it comes into question.

You may have set expectations for yourself, and now you feel you must live up to them. Are these expectations realistic? Healthy? Aligned with the person God created you to be?

Allow me to illustrate some examples of common places we find identity playing a large role.

What is a title- or position-based identity?

When I was in the United States Marine Corps, there was never a question of who was in charge at any given time. The ranks are clearly marked and known. Furthermore, when two or more are the same rank, seniority determines authority. As a young Lance Corporal, I was under the charge of the Corporal. My identity as a Lance Corporal determined my actions in obedience to the Corporal's every directive as well as those given by any rank above him in the chain of command. To be considered a "good Marine," my obedience would have to be prompt, excellent, and done without complaint. Being a "good Marine" was an identity on its own. When I was promoted to Corporal and later to Sergeant, my title-based identity changed. Those among whom I interacted had new expectations of me. In addition to complying with orders received from those whose ranks were above my own, I was expected to give orders to those in my charge. My identity grew from that of a follower into a leader, based solely on my position and title. This is an example of a title-based identity.

Identities defined in the context of one's role in the family are similar to title-based identities in some respects. As a child, we are expected to obey our parents without question. As we grow into young adulthood, we begin responding to outside influences more, such as peer pressure, etc. We then become adults and that identity moves us into independence. This identity can be challenged and sometimes overridden by parents who want their adult children to comply with their rules. But in general, the identity of adult independence is a natural course.

After independence, we take on the identity of spouse, which brings a new set of expectations. As a husband, I'm expected to love, protect, provide, and care for my wife. As my wife, she, in turn, accepts that part of her identity as a wife is to love, protect, provide, and care for me. While I used the same words relative to both of these roles, the application will usually be very different. For example, a husband may be expected to protect his wife physically while the wife may be expected to protect her husband from verbal accusations or gossip.

Each relationship will be different, but role-based identities are always present, and they control our actions. When we become parents, this new identity carries the expectation that we provide for our children, teach them right from wrong, and train them to be good citizens. Therefore, much like a job title identity, there is a natural progression to our roles within the family as we transition from one role and set of relationships to another.

Another identity that plays a role in the way we perceive ourselves is the identity anchored in location or origin. For example, when a tourist visits another land, he will introduce himself to others by identifying himself with a well-known location. A real-life application of this would be when I moved to Colorado from Hemet, California. Most people outside of the area immediately surrounding Hemet have no idea where it is. On the other hand, most people have heard of Riverside County, and almost everyone has heard of southern California. Therefore, when a conversation turns to where we moved from, I will say "We lived in Southern California... in a little town called Hemet in Riverside County." Therefore, I am identifying with a location that is well-known to answer a question or relate to someone.

However, some people place a high priority on their location identity. For example, someone from New York City may find ways to ensure everyone in a small country town knows they are from "the big city" and emphasize that fact as a distinguishing identity. Conversely, someone who currently resides in a city but was raised on a farm or ranch in the country may choose to distinguish himself by continuing to dress in a manner that accentuates or even exaggerates his "country-ness." These are examples of a location-based identity. Although these examples seem a little extreme, we have all probably met someone—and maybe even *been* someone—who uses location as a means to identify and display uniqueness.

Throughout this book, I will expand on several different types of identity. However, identity extends far beyond those represented by the examples I just provided. We assume many other types of identities, and we all have multiple identities that are constantly trying to assert a position of priority in our lives.

As I expand on these ideas and concepts, you may ask the question, "So what? Why is this important?"

The answer is relatively simple. The way we relate to our various identities can answer almost every question we have when it comes to why we do the things we do: some honorable, some irresponsible, some curious, some baffling, and some just downright strange. Depending on the hierarchy structure of our identities, they will directly impact certain areas of our lives. Each identity becomes so deeply rooted within us, it can directly affect our decisions, our trajectory, our success, and by extension, our health, our happiness, and so much more. It can mean the difference between establishing healthy relationships and continuing to attract toxic people into our lives. Perhaps most alarming, it can keep us stuck in a rut of making terrible decisions in various areas of our lives if we do not learn to recognize our various identities, gain perspective on their importance and their hold on us, and learn to manage them effectively by placing them in a hierarchy of proper priorities.

Maybe you're saying, "Hold on, Michael. You're trying to tell me my identity controls all that?" Yes, the truth of the matter is, it really is that important. Identity, as we will explore it throughout this book, manipulates a deep and vast web of various prompts, checks, balances, and experiences that are constantly vying with one another to take center stage. And you are the stage!

Allow me to refer to an earlier part of this chapter. Did you ever wonder why some people do strange things that don't seem to make sense? More to the point, have *you* ever taken action and done something while your conscience was screaming at you to do something else? Did you ever stop to consider why you did such a thing? Perhaps you were so committed to an argument that even when you realized you were wrong, you continued to argue. In another scenario, did your friends ever invite you (or dare you?) to do something that would make your parents puke at the thought of their precious baby engaging in such an act? Did you decide to take part, even when you didn't want to? Have you ever allowed an attractive salesperson to smooth-talk you into spending money you didn't intend to spend? Or worse, you went into debt for an item you really didn't need?

Unfortunately, we can all relate to at least one of these scenarios. These are actions prompted by an identity that should not be at the forefront of our minds, taking control of our decisions. My goal is to make these principles clear in the pages of this book.

Let's examine each of these scenarios more closely. You continue arguing even after you realize you are wrong because you consider yourself to be a smart person who is always right, and that identity is at stake. That identity will do whatever it takes to hold the top position, even if it means your proud, willful identity will dominate that of the kind person inside you—the one who is willing to admit when you are wrong.

Perhaps you joined your friends in using drugs in high school because being cool took precedence over your identity as someone who didn't do that stuff.

Finally, that attractive young salesperson approached you in the electronics center of the store and suddenly you realized you had just purchased more than you could afford. Did this come from your need to identify as wealthy or successful? When that identity of a successful image took over, it overrode your identity as the frugal person who is smart with money. It is no surprise that the best salespeople are skilled at appealing to the most flamboyant side of their customers. Once that appeal hits its target, the sale is in the bag! But I digress.

These examples may seem silly on the surface, but they highlight the importance of having positive identities that will overrule the negative ones. A positive or negative identity is not a matter of good or bad; rather, it is a matter of addition or subtraction. A positive identity is what you are, a negative identity is what you are not. Positive identities are much stronger than negative identities, as we will explore later in this book.

The fact is that these identities assert their influence over us every day, all across the world. Few dynamics exert a more powerful force in your life than those activated by your identity. It can be a motivator or an immobilizer. It can be the reason for your great success, or it can be the reason you keep engaging in self-defeating behaviors. This is real life, and this is a real-life issue.

When you become aware of the power of identities and you are confident in your ability to control them, you will be prepared to deal with big decisions more appropriately, perform better under pressure, and live a life free of restriction. You see, when your identities are wrongly prioritized, the ones that dominate have a way of restricting your movement. Oftentimes the expectations they place on you dictate standards and mindsets that you must live up to—some of which are simply unnecessary or even ridiculous!

Conversely, other identities set you free. These are the ones you must strive to nurture, protect, and maintain at the forefront of your life.

The highest identity that truly sets you free, of course, is your identity in Christ. When we place our identity in Christ at the top of your identity hierarchy, every decision or action must first be filtered through that identity. If we could live in a perfect world, this would be the ideal we would strive to achieve.

The reality is that most of us, if not all of us, walk a path that includes areas in our lives that are less than honorable in the sight of the Lord. The steps we have taken to create that beaten path speak volumes about priorities we have set, decisions we have made, and habits we have formed. In truth, the courses of action that mark our daily routines have reinforced our emerging identities. Conversely, the identities we have chosen to take priority in our daily lives are revealed in the courses of action we have pursued. The beauty of having a strong identity in Christ is that it not only makes decisions much easier and destroys bad habits; it also sets us free from the condemnation that comes from making those mistakes and wrong choices and allows us to move on when we make the wrong decisions. Isn't that just awesome? But how do we get there?

A sobering word of caution here: the other identities don't go away when you have chosen to walk with the Lord and have established an identity in Christ. They absolutely will not go away. Even Jesus had identities outside of His identity as the Christ. He was a carpenter from Nazareth, a son, a friend, and He was a human. Nevertheless, the various identities you have are not something to be despised or looked down upon. That said, they must be assigned to their rightful place, *below* your identity in Christ. So as we explore this concept in the next few chapters, we will define the various types of identities, learn ways to recognize them, and discover ways they can be implemented to become a better version of ourselves.

From the moment He designed you as a unique person and created you with care and love, He intended for you to live a life free of the stress imposed by the conflicting identities that vie for control of your mind and your heart. You deserve to live a life defined by His unique calling and is free of the stressors that such conflicts impose.

Let's discover the joys of this life together.

2
TITLE IDENTITIES

FOR EVERYTHING IN THE WORLD – THE LUST OF THE FLESH, THE LUST OF THE EYES, AND THE PRIDE OF LIFE – COMES NOT FROM THE FATHER BUT FROM THE WORLD. THE WORLD AND ITS DESIRES PASS AWAY, BUT WHOEVER DOES THE WILL OF GOD LIVES FOREVER.
1 JOHN 2:16-17

Jarod walks through the doors of a multi-level corporate building for a job interview with a prestigious firm. His impressive resume, highlighting his experience and education, should make him an excellent candidate for this job. Although he is confident, his stomach churns a little bit every time he has to do something like this. As he approaches the elevator, he is halted by a security guard.

"I haven't seen you before," says the security guard. His speech is delivered in a dull, even tone as if he could fall asleep at any time.

"I have a job interview on the 5th floor," Jarod says quickly as he turns toward the elevator.

"Whoa, hold on a minute." The security guard's voice picks up a little this time. "I need to issue you a visitor's pass."

"Ugh. Seriously? I might be late to the interview," Jarod replies, clearly flustered. This isn't the truth. He has made a point to arrive well before the scheduled time because he's eager to impress the interviewers.

"Rules are rules, my friend," says the guard, as he sits behind a computer to start the process, resuming his even, boring tone of voice.

"Wow," is all Jarod can say. Shifting from one foot to the other as he waits, his frustration continues to grow at the thought of having to comply with such a seemingly unimportant point of protocol.

The security guard looks up from his computer with a hint of a smirk. Apparently, he finds Jarod's frustration amusing. This infuriates Jarod. *Wow, who does this security guard think he is?* Jarod fumes. *He obviously has a pretty high opinion of himself and enjoys abusing what little power he has. It must be so satisfying to this little cop-wannabe to throw a monkey wrench in someone's day. The nerve of this guy!* As these thoughts whirl around in Jarod's head, the security guard takes his sweet time issuing the pass to check him in.

"Good luck with your interview," says the guard with a smile as he hands Jarod his driver's license and guest-pass.

Was that sarcasm? Jarod snatches the cards, mutters "Thanks," and rushes over to the elevator to go up to the 5th floor.

Although most of you who read this probably have a high level of respect for security guards, this type of interaction is not uncommon. Let's say the person interviewing Jarod is the CFO of the company. Can you imagine Jarod going into his job interview with the same attitude when speaking to the CFO? Of course not. Because the title of CFO conveys importance, power, influence, and the ability to decide Jarod's future with the company. So if there is a difference between the way he treats a security guard and the way he would interact with the CFO, what does that say about how he sees them? Does he look at them as individuals who deserve respect just because they are people, or does he only consider them in terms of the title each one holds? You know the answer, of course. Jarod is doing what many of us do every day. He is assigning value to each person based on their title.

Jarod believes he can be rude to the security guard for two reasons:

1. He does not hold a high position of authority.

2. He has no real influence, nor is he a decision-maker with any control over whether or not Jarod gets the job.

If we attach too much importance on titles, we will ask two questions about every person we meet:

1. Who are they? –Or– Are they a person of influence, power, or prestige?

2. What can they do for me, or what can they restrict me from?

Title identities are probably the biggest category of identities we have. Attaching a great deal of importance to our title identity simply reveals that we use our title, our field, or our job description to define our value. One indicator that a person has a strong title identity is that they will often find ways to bring up their title in conversation.

Finding identity in titles is not necessarily a bad thing. Quite the opposite. It's necessary for many normal functions of life. However, like all things, when placed in an incorrect priority, a focus on one's title identity can be destructive. We use them in various ways. For example, organizational titles such as CEO, president, manager, or supervisor, or job descriptions like security guard, banker, graphic designer, market-er, and so on—these label the roles we play in an organization or the job descriptions to which we conform. Throughout this book, when I mention titles or title identities, I am referring to the entire category defined here. These are all title identities, and they can often become our primary definition of who we are and who others see us as.

Title identities can be attained through accomplishments, seniority, education, or force. Let's take a closer look at each of these dynamics.

When the Denver Broncos finally won the Super Bowl in 1997, John Elway lifted the Lombardi trophy over his head. In a single day, that accomplishment determined his title and legacy. He went from being a great quarterback in the National Football League to a Super Bowl Champion quarterback. That accomplishment not only changed his title, but also changed the title of the franchise as it was their first Super Bowl win. The Denver Broncos were now Super Bowl Champions. This is an accomplishment-based title.

Next is the seniority-based title. If you have spent any length of time in the workforce, you have probably encountered a job where seniority was a factor that carried a lot of weight when being considered for a promotion. For example, if I've only been on the job for six months and I receive direction from someone who has been on the job for five years, I will probably submit to their authority, based on their seniority. In this case, if for no other reason, their title as a senior worker carries authority because they have been there longer, and they probably know the job better than I do.

Titles based on seniority are found in education, too. As you go through high school, as long as you do not mess up, by year four, you will receive the title of senior. To some extent, this title is linked to your accomplishments. However, barring some really poor decisions or inadequacies, you will automatically be promoted from freshman to sophomore to junior to senior based on time alone—and seniority. At the end of your four-year journey, you will have earned the title of high school graduate. This brings us to the educational title.

Education title identity is just that: finding your identity in your educational title. I'll go more into this concept in the next chapter, but I'll open up the idea here. For instance, someone who has graduated with a bachelor's degree has achieved the title of college graduate. Some people place a high priority on their educational title and use it as a framework to determine the way they value others and their opinions. When engaged in a discussion with someone who is a college dropout—or who has never gone to college—they may adopt a disparaging attitude toward that person, dismissing their opinions as less informed or less important because of their lack of education.

When I was in college, I had many professors who achieved the titles of Ph.D. through education. I recall one professor in particular who frequently inserted and asserted his title when giving a lecture or leading a discussion. On one occasion, I did not agree with his opinion on a matter that was open to debate. Adopting an argumentative stance, his winning argument was, "I know my opinion is correct because I'm a doctor, and you are not." I am not embellishing this story in any way; this really happened. I am not a naturally gifted debater, nor do I seek confrontation, so I let it go.

Of course, his point is easily tossed out when all I need to do is find someone with a Ph.D. like himself who disagrees with him. That professor's line of thinking says, "When I earn my Ph.D., then my opinion will matter more than anyone else's." How absurd to maintain that an opinion does not matter on its own merit; that its merit is determined based on the educational title of the one giving the opinion. This is an example of someone who places a high value on—and assigns a high priority to—their educational title identity.

Furthermore, many people believe their opinion in any given argument should prevail based on their title. This, of course, is ludicrous. If a title is the determining factor in a debate, all you would have to do to refute the "winning" argument would be to find someone of an equal or higher title to disagree with them. Even so, many people subscribe to this mindset and value someone's opinion based largely on their title rather than the merit of the opinion.

Finally, titles can be taken by force. However, if we do take a title by force, we may well find that we will also have to defend such a title by force. This is not as common in our culture today as it was in times past, so I'll establish this point in a historical context. In Judges chapter 9, we read the story of Abimelech, the son of Gideon. Abimelech had 70 brothers whose birthright was higher than his own. Therefore, his brothers had a stronger claim to the seat of leadership over Israel. However, Abimelech decided that he would be the ruler. How did he achieve this? Through force. The townspeople gave him money, which he used to "hire reckless scoundrels" (verse 4), and after enlisting the financial support of his clansmen, a posse of mercenaries went out and killed all his brothers. Only his brother Jotham escaped. Unfortunately, as we read through the rest of chapter 9, we see that Abimelech's rule was one riddled with conflict and was only maintained through constant use of force. Unable to let his guard down, he constantly had to fight to defend his right to rule. This exemplifies how, when we take a title by force, we usually have to defend it by force.

Next, let's take a look at a more practical side of title identity.

Titles help us know what to expect from others. They provide us with an expectation of the role that person will play or what that person will provide for us. Often, we take this a step further. Consciously or subconsciously, that person's title acts as a lens that determines what we anticipate in terms of the quality of their service. For example, if my wife and I were seeking marital counseling, we might ask our pastor to do the job, thinking that his title conveyed a certain depth of training, experience, and knowledge in this area (an expectation based on the title). On the other hand, if the lead pastor referred us to an elder in the church—one we didn't even know held the position of elder—rather than allowing us to counsel with the pastor, we might underestimate the value of the elder's counsel, thinking that his title didn't carry the same weight as the title of pastor. The title – elder – might not give us confidence that he would be adequate to the task (an expectation of quality based on the title). This, of course, is not always a good means of determining the quality of service one has to offer. That elder might have been placed in that position for a reason, and might even have greater insight and more experience in counseling couples. Although it is not always an accurate measure, we rely heavily on titles when formulating our expectations of others.

Another aspect of title identities is found in the expectations we place on ourselves. Our titles can dramatically affect our way of life, the things we do, and the things we feel responsible for. In the enlisted ranks of the military, there are junior enlisted ranks (lowest), non-commissioned officers (NCOs), and staff non-commissioned officers (staff NCOs, the highest). As a junior-enlisted rank, my title said I must follow the directions of all NCOs and staff NCOs. Although I may have had a title of authority similar to an NCO, such as watch-leader, my primary title as a junior enlisted was my charge. This title meant I was responsible to do my job, work hard, be excellent, and follow the directions of the NCOs. In general, if I did something wrong, the NCOs above me would be held accountable by the staff-NCOs. The NCOs would then hold me accountable. This is how the chain of command is supposed to work.

However, when I became an NCO, the things expected of me changed, and my personal expectations and actions changed. I was no longer responsible for only my actions; I was then also responsible for the actions of the junior enlisted under my charge. Although I hadn't changed as a person, my title had changed. And as we have explored, titles carry expectations with them. In addition, they usually affect the way we act and the expectations we place on ourselves. As an NCO, I no longer had the liberty to be close friends with junior enlisted ranks. At least not on the same level as before, because that would have been considered fraternization. I then had to find ways to motivate those under my charge to do excellent work. Furthermore, because I was held responsible for their work as well as my own, I needed to check the quality of their work as well as my own. I would then report to the staff-NCO. For this reason, I adopted practices, rituals, and habits that equipped me to live up to my new title most effectively. For example, when leading others in fitness routines, I would have to step up my game in my personal fitness routines.

Someone who places the weight of their identity in titles will appear strongly driven. They often allow their title to be a driving force for their ambitions. Military service is the best example I can use to illustrate this point because the titles that delineate the chain of command in various branches of the military are clearly marked and universally understood. Let me explain. In the Marine Corps, a promotion is earned by attaining a high composite score. Elements that figure into that score include physical fitness, continuing education, and personal evaluations. So to achieve the highest possible composite score when I was a Lance Corporal in the Marines (a junior-enlisted rank), I pushed myself in each of these areas, striving for a high level of physical fitness, pursuing continuing education, and earning high marks on my evaluations. I didn't do these things because I loved physical fitness or Math for Marines; rather, I pursued these disciplines because I desired to rise to the rank of Corporal. My desire for the higher title drove me to achieve higher levels of performance. This doesn't mean I wouldn't have done an excellent job otherwise (and for other identity reasons), but the truth is that title ambition was a big factor in my striving so hard to attain my goals.

Finding identity in your title is not necessarily a bad thing when placed in a proper perspective. But we have all seen that person who is so focused on impressing the boss and securing the next promotion that he seems to care little about the people around him. He may be a very caring person in other dimensions of his life, but because he attaches so much importance to securing a higher title, seeking that promotion has come to dominate his every inclination and dwarfs the importance he attaches to the way he treats his peers.

What can go wrong?

Title identities are not inherently wrong, but they can be dangerous if misused or assigned a wrong priority. Leadership may misuse the title identity of their subordinate leaders. For example, imagine upper management in a company imploring the financial manager to submit better reports. One of the responsibilities that come with being the financial manager is an expectation to improve the company's numbers. However, what if the company is currently going through a downturn in growth. If that manager struggles with his title identity, he may be tempted to adjust the numbers to make himself and the company look good. In this scenario, upper management may be setting unfair expectations on the financial manager based on his title. Furthermore, the financial manager has mis-prioritized this part of his identity. If he adjusts the numbers to look better, he is doing so to protect the title identity that tells him and his supervisors he is responsible to submit good reports. If he doesn't submit a good report, he is not living up to the expectations he associates with his title identity (whether he put those expectations on himself or not). In so doing, he places his title identity above his identity as an honest person.

Although this is a fictitious illustration, it exemplifies the devastating effects that can result if we distort the priority we attach to our titles. I used to love watching the sitcom "The Office." The butt of many jokes in that show was a man named Dwight. Dwight was a stickler for following rules, respecting authority, and a very hard worker. The regional manager, Michael, gave Dwight the title of assistant to the regional manager. Did this title carry a higher pay rate than that of his peers? No. Did he have any additional authority other than what he perceived as his own importance? No. So why was this title so important to him? Because he derived a lot of his identity from his title. Therefore, when his boss gave him a nice title, the benefits of said title were irrelevant. The title itself was enough to satisfy Dwight.

Although this is a fictitious and comedic story, you probably know someone like Dwight at your workplace. Dwight is a caricature of a real-life type of person who so highly values titles.

An employer who understands the powerful effect of title identities can use them to recognize, motivate, control, or elevate an employee with little risk or investment. Most of you who are reading this have probably experienced or witnessed a "promotion" that awarded the promoted worker a new title without a change in pay.

Sometimes we may ask why an employer would do such a thing. The three-part answer is simple. Let's use our example of Dwight. First, if Dwight places a high value on titles, that simple title upgrade is enough to keep him happy for a time without a pay increase. Second, the employer can ask more of Dwight now because the title involves additional responsibilities and expectations. Third, if the new title boosts Dwight's morale, he may work harder or uphold a higher standard. Of course, a promotion without a pay increase is not always backed by a devious plan. However, this illustrates how an employer could easily use title identity as a means of manipulation.

Another aspect to consider is the ability to *sell* a title. Someone who places a high value on titles may pay a high price to attain a title that glimmers with prestige. Think about a certificate that gives you a title, but does not actually give you any additional level of expertise. Or consider an honorary degree awarded a generous donor. Whether or not such a degree is deserved is debatable, but as you explore the purpose of such a degree, awarding the degree is a way of honoring the recipient with a title which the giver is at liberty to bestow.

And then there are the titles we pay for with money. Intelligent marketers know the value of titles. They appeal to our innate desire to be recognized, prized, and honored above others. This can come in many forms. For example, a business coach might attach a higher price to a product or service he offers without actually increasing its value. By declaring the material "exclusive" or designating it for his VIPs or his "inner circle," he establishes a greater perceived value, when it costs him little or nothing to do so. The aspects of selling a title are usually hidden, but it is a very real part of our lives in western culture.

But why do I say placing too much identity in our title can be dangerous?

The pursuit and maintenance of a title can become exhausting and eventually consume our very being. The reality is this: you can never reach the pinnacle of titles in life. There will always be something more to chase after and something further to achieve. As you realize you are in a never-ending game of chase, stress levels are bound to rise. As you gaze at that title you so desperately want, glittering in the distance, and you realize how far you are from making it your own, you may start to devalue yourself. Furthermore, you may question your intelligence, your gifts, or your abilities.

When your value, worth, and identity are intricately enmeshed to your title, you will feel like less of a person anytime you interact with someone who holds a higher title. Much like the professor who believes the fact that he holds a Ph.D. makes his opinion more valuable than anyone who lacks that level of achievement. If my identity were heavily tied into my title, I might accept or even adopt his assessment that his title gives him a badge of unquestionable intelligence. Then by default, I would have to accept that my opinion was less valuable—or perhaps even that my intrinsic worth as a person was diminished—just because I lacked that title.

This is a sad place to live.

Unfortunately, many people allow themselves to become trapped in the mindset that their title—or lack thereof—is a pitiful but indisputable declaration that *they are not enough.* Furthermore, they look at others of higher titles as more valuable than themselves.

Again, this is a sad and dangerous place to live. If you constantly find yourself competing with other people based on their titles, you will relish any chance you get to assert your dominance over others based on your title alone. This is where we get the expression that the promotion "went to their head" or became a "power trip."

All of this may sound negative, but there is definitely a positive side to this question of titles. There are very clear-cut reasons for titles to exist. A title may convey experience, education, and skills. They allow us to assign leadership and expectations of responsibility.

Let's go back to my military example. The various ranks make it clear who is in command in any given situation. This is, of course, helpful in a workforce. Titles provide clarity and security in a world of confusion. As such, they help us ensure order in a civilized society. Therefore, a title in and of itself usually has value, and it can be used for the good.

That said, we must always be aware that there are those who place too much of their identity in their title. At the very least, this contributes to a misaligned valuation of oneself and others. Furthermore, it often sets them up for manipulation, power struggles, and exhausting ambition.

God does not want us to derive our self-worth from our titles, nor does He want us to assign the worth of others based on theirs. This is why He constantly opposed the Pharisees, who rooted their identity in their religious titles. Jesus did not devalue those whom society labeled as unimportant. He saw people as children of God, which awarded them equal standing with every other human. When we find our identity in Christ, we can humbly accept the value He places on us rather than trying vainly to attain value on our own through worldly identities. In that humility, we learn that others have the same value as we do, as children of God. Not more, not less, but the same.

An identity in Christ gives humility, and true humility rests in the knowledge of true worth defined by Jesus' sacrifice on the cross.

3

EDUCATION IDENTITIES

DO NOT DECEIVE YOURSELVES. IF ANY OF YOU THINK YOU ARE WISE BY
THE STANDARDS OF THIS AGE, YOU SHOULD BECOME "FOOLS" SO
THAT YOU MAY BECOME WISE.
1 CORINTHIANS 3:18

Most people will agree education is a good thing. It provides an environment for a foundation of learning. Formal education gives people a structured road map to success and hope for job security. And it provides a means by which we can benchmark the basic expectations of society (e.g., we can all agree on the times tables, etc.).

But what does it mean to find your identity in your education? That simply means that you expect your level of education to speak to others about who you are. Furthermore, you may form your opinion of someone's value around their level of education.

Now when I put it that way, it automatically seems a bad thing. However, as I have mentioned, and as we will continue to discuss in this book, we have multiple identities. Rest assured, finding one part of your identity in your education is not a bad thing in itself. However, misplacing any part of your identity will have negative results.

There are many forms of education. However, for the points made in this chapter, when I speak of education, I am generally referring to formal schooling from kindergarten through college. As you read through the chapter, please keep these parameters in mind.

Why do people get an education? Furthermore, why do some pursue a series of advanced degrees and educational titles?

Although there are other identities at play of higher priority than educational titles, the reason is often rooted in their educational identity.

When I say there are other identities at play, I mean educational identity is usually not at the top of the identity hierarchy, rather it is a means to fulfilling a higher identity pursuit.

For example, let's say my highest identity is found in the amount of money I earn. That being the case, my focus is on earning a high income. If I believe that working as an accountant for a big company would earn a high income, I would pursue higher education to become an accountant. Therefore, education is the means by which I can fulfill my higher identity needs.

Again, education is not a bad thing. However, as people climb the educational ladder, they often compare themselves to those who have not achieved their level of educational success and develop a spirit of pride and superiority. This is when it gets dicey.

Let's go over some of the great benefits and importance of education. The first and most obvious is the standardization of basic educational requirements for children. For the most part, we learn the basic skills of arithmetic, language, grammar, reading, writing, and science at a young age.

It is quite useful to live in a society where you can generally be confident in the public's ability to read and do basic math. Furthermore, when we meet another adult, we can usually assume that person has at least a high school education. To some extent, this is useful when having a conversation or when forming expectations of a person based on that assumption.

Another reason education is important is to learn specific skills and gain credibility in a field. We can probably agree that there should be some regulation in certain fields. The medical field is an example of a line of work that absolutely requires the credibility earned through extensive education.

However, credibility may also be attained based on the public's perception of value added through education. For example, some people would not be comfortable following a pastor who did not go through seminary before becoming the pastor of their church. Therefore, the seminary degree gives that pastor credibility with people who consider that level of education to be important. It is also a selling point that can give confidence to the educated individual. For example, a Ph.D. may feel more confident writing a book and marketing it because their degree adds credibility when attached to their name on the spine. They could market their book based on the notion that the public will assume they must know what they are talking about if they have achieved a doctorate. Therefore, their educational level is a validation of their credibility based on public perception.

I once had a professor tell me a degree will not make me more skilled in a given area of expertise, but it is indicative of the type of person who attained the degree: they set a goal, engaged in the disciplines required to attain that goal, and saw the goal through to completion.

For this reason, when a person is being considered for a position, a degree can set them apart from the crowd as someone who, at a minimum, was self-motivated enough to see something through.

That brings me to the next benefit of formal education. Education is often a great tool to get a job. This is not only the most obvious reason for pursuing higher education, it is often the primary one. We are all familiar with the mantra: "Do good in school, get an education, and get a good job." This career advice comprises the common paradigm that most people live by in western culture and is generally an accepted way of life.

Therefore, there are many benefits to attaining higher levels of formal education. Furthermore, it may be comforting to know all of the benefits of having a higher education can be attained and enjoyed without education becoming a significant identity in someone's life. This means you can pursue and attain educational titles and accomplishments without finding your identity and value in them. On the other hand, it also doesn't mean you can't find identity in your education. But like other identities, if placed in too high a priority, educational titles can breed a spirit of pride.

Let's talk further about the effects of placing your educational identity in the wrong priority. Sometimes this becomes evident early on in a person's life. Were your parents so focused on your grades that it seemed they cared little about anything else you accomplished? Such an attitude can instill a warped view in young children about where their value comes from. Before long, they conclude that poor grades in school means they are "less than" others or not as smart as others. Even the most well-meaning parents who want the best for their children can fall into this trap without realizing the effect it has on their children. Whether this attitude is instilled in children by their parents or by someone in the school system, a hypersensitivity to grade achievement leaves children with the impression that any sense of love, acceptance, respect, or personal worth is directly dependent upon their performance in school. This leads them to associate their educational accomplishments with who they are and where their value comes from.

The worst part about this is that it doesn't matter if the child does well or poorly in school; they all get the same message when grades are overemphasized. The child with poor grades will develop low self-esteem and accept his or her value as less than that of the "smart" kids. The child with high grades will become prideful, root their sense of self-worth in that achievement, and begin to expect others to respect them based on those grades. It should come as no surprise that this forms a mindset that they carry throughout life.

Another negative side-effect that can occur when grades and education are too highly valued is that actual learning takes a back seat. This has many negative effects, including cheating.

Think about it. Why do people cheat on exams, anyway?

I have a theory that a person cheats because he values the appearance of being a good student above learning the subject matter. Therefore, cheating is often the predictable result of a student wanting to appear a good student rather than adopting the actual work and study habits of a good student.

In the end, what good is passing a test if one doesn't learn the material?

Think about the courses you went through in school. How often was the teacher "teaching the test" and ensuring the students memorized certain points so they could pass the test?

Sadly, this is the state many students find themselves in, however self-imposed it may be. I'm not suggesting grades are not important. These examples are to show how an identity rooted in grades can lead a student down the wrong path in the course of pursuing their education.

Once again, I want to be clear. There is nothing wrong with pursuing formal education and striving for high grades. Education is very important and in many areas, nothing short of vital. Furthermore, while one's level of education does not always equate to intellect, it is often a reliable indicator of it. The point of this chapter is not to suggest that education is unimportant; rather, it is to demonstrate the need to place education in a proper priority and to warn you not to allow your education to become your main identity. Furthermore, it's quite important to maintain an appropriately humble view of others who have not achieved an educational level that matches your own.

As children of God, we know He will give us wisdom if we ask (James 1:5). Furthermore, the Bible tells us in Proverbs 2:6 "All wisdom comes from the Lord, and so do common sense and understanding" (CEV). Therefore, we know where our wisdom comes from. It comes from Christ.

This understanding brings about true identity in Christ. As His child, you can trust that He is reliable and faithful enough to give you wisdom and understanding. It is not your education that will further your wisdom and give you more authority. If you root your identity in your education rather than in the true Educator, you will never achieve true wisdom—because that only comes from God.

If you believe your authority and value comes from education, you have made education an idol.

Sure, you can argue that God will use your education for the advancement of His Kingdom, but that cannot come at the expense of relying on your education to save you and provide for your soul needs.

Your education should not define who you are as a Christian. If you are a follower of Christ, identity in Him is the only thing that defines your value.

Maybe you're thinking, "Now this all sounds fine and dandy, but aren't you just giving lazy people an excuse to continue being lazy?"

On the contrary! Identity in Christ in no way diminishes the value of your education or your drive to pursue further education. What it does mitigate is your desire to attain education with the intent to establish superiority over others to prove others wrong.

Identity in Christ will enhance all forms of education and allow you to truly excel in the application of the benefits of that education.

What do I mean?

When we can freely pursue Christ, He reveals to us areas of education we should pursue and excel in.

In the New Testament, Jesus called us salt and light (Matthew 5:13-14). Does salt diminish the flavor of food? No way! I put salt on food that is bland to enhance the natural flavors that are already there!

In the same way, does light hide things when the switch is turned on? Of course not! It illuminates and brings to life the things that were previously hard to see.

In this same way, when you seek the wisdom of God and not that of humans, the natural wisdom of the World becomes much more clear and useful. Furthermore, confidence in who you are in Christ allows you to learn freely from the World without anchoring your worth in what your peers or teachers think about you. Your value is found in what God thinks about you, not the grades you earn on a man-made test.

After all, Christ finds you valuable enough to die for.

With that knowledge, how could you ever allow someone to question your value based on your level of education, your perceived intellect, or the grade you got on a test? In fact, if someone disparages your value, they are not insulting you as much as they are insulting God. After all, God is the one who decided you were worth dying for, not you.

It is important to note here that if you use this knowledge without wisdom, it can lead to arrogance. And that is the opposite of true identity in Christ. Jesus died on the cross for you and every other human being on the planet. Therefore, when you look down on another based on their level of education, you are walking down a path of self-reliance—a choice that is offensive towards God. Don't take this as condemnation because we've all done it at some point.

I realize I've made a few hard statements in this chapter that may go against the grain or may even feel condemning. Condemnation is not my goal, rather I'm bringing to the light what I believe to be the truth based on what the Bible says. If you think about it from the perspective that your value is found in Christ's sacrifice, not in your earthly achievements, you cannot conclude that anything else could possibly determine your true worth.

Again, education is not a bad thing when viewed in its proper context, kept in perspective, and assigned its proper priority. And as we pursue an education, we must remain mindful that true wisdom only comes from God.

I implore you to continue to seek the Lord in this journey and to realize your worth in Him is not determined by any initials at the end of your name. Although they are significant in this life and He will use them to His glory, they will not make you more valuable as a child of God.

4

IDENTITY IN ACCOMPLISHMENTS

WHAT GOOD IS IT FOR SOMEONE TO GAIN THE WHOLE WORLD, AND
YET LOSE OR FORFEIT THEIR VERY SELF?
LUKE 9:25

Accomplishments are hills we climb along our walk of life. Sometimes chosen, sometimes necessary, they elevate us for a short time in our journey toward a larger goal. A significant accomplishment can bring a sense of elation. It's okay to camp out on such an accomplishment hill for a short time, but these hills are not designed for us to stay there.

As some of you may know, Marine Corps recruit training (boot camp) is a grueling 13-week program designed to shift a person's mental and physical makeup completely. It alters who they are and how they see themselves. One of the most physically demanding points during that 13 weeks is a pinnacle of testing known as the Crucible. The Crucible consists of three days and three nights of mental and physical exhaustion. In those three days, recruits walk a distance of about 40 miles with a 40- to 60-pound backpack and an M16 rifle, occasionally stopping for various combat-style exercises and physical tests. The only break they get in each 24-hour period is a four-hour stint during which they must set up and tear down their tents, stand fire watch, and catch whatever time to sleep that they can in between.

Each recruit is issued 1.5 packaged meals. Not 1.5 meals per day; 1.5 meals for the entire three-day Crucible.

At the end of the Crucible comes the ultimate test of strength and fortitude called the Reaper. About two-thirds of the way through a 10-mile hike, the Reaper is about a half-mile stretch of steep vertical climb/hike. Remember, this is after three days of exhaustion. Before making the ascent, recruits are allowed about 10 minutes at the bottom to rest, use the porta-potty, and take a few sips from their canteen. Once they reach the top of the Reaper, the recruits gather and experience a momentary shift in the way they are treated by their drill instructors.

Why the shift in the way recruits are treated by the drill instructors?

You see, the Crucible is a rite of passage into the Marine Corps. After completing this grueling test, they emerge as United States Marines. With that accomplishment under his belt, one is no longer a recruit – he is now a Marine.

The accomplishment is significant. However, as great an achievement as it is, it does not encompass all that a Marine is. It only marks one of the first major milestones of his journey to become a full-fledged Marine.

Some of us seek accomplishments to validate who we are. But accomplishments are not meant to be identities in and of themselves. Accomplishments are simply building blocks and puzzle pieces that fit together to form the whole person we become.

To return to the metaphor of climbing a hill, each accomplishment is but one milestone on the journey that charts the course of your development. If that milestone figures into a broader sense of your calling, it advances you toward a solidification of who you are called to be.

Some people identify so much with their accomplishments, they may live in the past or get caught in the trap of forever chasing that high of accomplishing something new.

But note: accomplishments should be a result of who we are – or who you are becoming – not the other way around.

You need to understand this principle because it will liberate you from basing your worth on things you can achieve. What you achieve does become a part of who you are, but it does not *define* who you are. It may be a springboard into a new identity – a rite of passage – but it does not encompass the fullness of that identity.

I loved Legos as a child. I envisioned myself to be a grand architect building huge structures, lands, and castles with a bunch of little pieces all combined in the perfect order. I think of accomplishments like Lego pieces. A grand Lego structure is made of hundreds or thousands of small and large pieces that all fit together to design something significant. A single Lego by itself is useless, no matter the size. Accomplishments are like one big Lego that helps you get closer to building the entire Lego structure. They are designed to be built upon – they are not the entire structure.

Accomplishments have many good merits. Someone who is motivated by accomplishments will work hard in their pursuit of the next accomplishment. The ability to say one completed a tough task is a great feeling. On the road toward an accomplishment, we often find ourselves becoming better, stronger, and smarter people based on the experience. At the end of a long and grueling journey, the feeling of achievement is grand. It is a good thing to celebrate our accomplishments along the way. However, the glitter of accomplishments fades as the realities of life present us with the next thing to be accomplished, and the next....

Accomplishments are like checkpoints: points in time that mark off individual chapters of a life. They are the peaks overlooking the valleys of life. But as much as we would like to plant a flag on each hilltop and bask in the glory, we cannot establish residence on those accomplishment hills after planting the flag.

How silly would it have been during the Crucible for me to say, "I love this feeling of being at the top of the Reaper. I think I'll just stay here for the rest of my life."

If, in some alternate reality, I was allowed to do such a thing, would that be a good place for me to live? I mean, after all, I reached the goal of becoming a Marine—something that would be with me forever, right? And how much higher could I go than achieving that status? Furthermore, now that I had earned the title of Marine, did I need to do anything else to maintain that title? I think I should just stay at the top of that hill.

You're probably mentally screaming at me how silly this suggestion sounds. However, we are all guilty of doing this very thing at some point in our personal walks through life. We try to claim glory over and over again after a big competition win, promotion, graduation, or some other significant life event.

With the Crucible example, you can see how silly it is to try to live on top of an accomplishment hill.

What if I had stayed on the top of that hill (the Reaper) until the end of my five-year enlistment period? When I exited the Marine Corps, someone might ask, "So, what did you do in the Marines?"

"Well, I went to boot camp, and after completing the Crucible, and climbing the Reaper, I became a Marine."

They would say, "No, I mean, what did you do after boot camp while you were in?"

"I stayed on the Reaper."

"What? Why would you go through all that just to stay on that hill?"

"Well, you see, the top of the Reaper is where we get our Eagle Globe & Anchor, and then we're awarded the title of United States Marine. Why would I need to continue to prove myself by doing anything else in the Marines? After all, I'm just as much a Marine as the other guy who went on to war during the years I was living on that hill, right?"

At that point, the person asking the questions would walk away, convinced they were talking to a crazy man.

Accomplishments, achievements, and rites of passage are not meant to be a place where we stay, either mentally or physically. Furthermore, they are not intended to define who we are. Yes, they validate us at critical points along our journey, and they can mark crucial stages of our development, but they are not to *define* who we are.

Someone who tries to live on top of an accomplishment will find that the sense of glory fades. Furthermore, accomplishments can become redundant. Generally speaking, an accomplishment leads to a title. That title usually becomes redundant if you achieve it twice. For example, if I were to go through boot camp again, I would achieve the same goal of becoming a Marine. When we look at it that way, it seems ridiculous. However, some people achieve an accomplishment and want to achieve it again. They continually seek that high of meeting that goal. Rather than considering accomplishments to be experiences that trace their progress on a journey, they think of it as an end in itself.

Furthermore, if one places too high a priority on accomplishments, they will always look back into their past to try to regain the sense of euphoria attached to that which is gone or has faded. At some point, you have to stop using the fact that you won the high school state championship in 1994 as the focal point of every conversation and the life achievement that validates your existence. Were you the valedictorian of your senior class? Did you graduate from a well-respected college? Did you organize a mission trip where 1,000 people gave their lives to Christ? Don't get me wrong—these are great accomplishments! However, they are not *who you are*. The merit of the accomplishment doesn't change the principle. Accomplishments are hills you climbed on your way to becoming the person you are today.

Some people's hills are higher than others, but they are only hills along a journey. Trying to hold on to those hills is not only ridiculous; it's impossible because we're living in the realm of time. Time always carries us forward; it does not allow us to take up residence on a hill of achievement. We can insist on standing proudly beside the flag we have planted, but as time marches on, it will always bring us back to reality.

As I've already pointed out, accomplishments are like hills we climb along life's journey.

At certain times in our lives, we will climb many hills of accomplishment, some higher than others. We must be careful when at the top of those hills not to look with disdain on others in the valley below. This is one reason people get stuck after anchoring their identity in accomplishments. Once they have done something they consider rather unique, the temptation might be to look down at others who chose to stay in the valley, rather than brave the same attempt. At that point, a feeling of superiority and pride may well up inside them. If that feeling of superiority gives them a rush, they might begin to crave that feeling and continue to look down on others who do not measure up in their eyes as achievers.

This mentality is recognizable in the conversations we have. Someone who has anchored their identity in accomplishments will find ways to insert it in any interaction. They do this because their accomplishments have become the identity that makes them feel valuable.

Furthermore, they will use accomplishments as a means to assess the value of others.

It is reasonable to use accomplishments to validate titles, positions, or awards. However, they do not define your value as a person. More specifically, they do not validate your value as a child of God.

As Christians, the things we set out to accomplish may look the same as the world, but our value and worth should not come from them. Although we may achieve the same results of the world, our primary focus is not on what we accomplish here. There is only one accomplishment worth finding your value in, and that is Jesus' victory over sin by His death on the cross. With that accomplishment, the whole world was granted freedom through His sacrifice. This freedom does not come at a cost to you and me; it is a free gift.

Furthermore, no accomplishment we can attain here on Earth can secure any more or less of that gift. The title 'child of God' is yours upon receiving and accepting that gift. That title is a "you do, or you don't," or "you are, or you aren't." There are no varying levels to being a follower of Christ; you either are, or you aren't. You have either accepted Christ into your life, or you have not. Furthermore, either you have submitted your life fully to Him, or you have not.

There is nothing you can accomplish here on Earth that will make you more of a child of God. There is nothing you can do to make yourself more valuable to Him.

Paul is a perfect example of focusing only on Jesus' accomplishment on the cross. If anyone could have boasted about his accomplishments during his life as a believer, it was Paul, one of the greatest apostles on the planet. He started a huge movement of God and planted many churches in a culture where this idea was not only rejected; those who followed it were persecuted. Today we get excited about hundreds of people being saved – but Paul brought entire cities to Jesus!

However, he never gloried in those mighty accomplishments to validate who he was. The words he used to begin every letter reveal where he found his identity: "Paul, an apostle of Jesus Christ." He knew his identity was not to be found in his worldly accomplishments, whether those achievements were righteous or not.

However, in the end, he told Timothy, "I have fought the good fight, I have finished the race" (2 Timothy 4:7). Secure in the knowledge that his identity and salvation were in Christ alone, he still fought the good fight. He was not content to simply lie down and submit his life to the rule and culture of the land. His identity in Christ gave him the power to speak the truth and act in truth.

Although I say there are no varying levels of being a Christ-follower, there *are* varying levels of how fulfilling your life as a Christian will be.

Paul, of course, is not the only one who exemplified the Christian life for us in the Bible.

The greatest example is Jesus himself. Jesus had the greatest achievement a human has ever had. After living a sinless life, He sacrificed Himself for us on the cross. In that one act, He both submitted Himself to the physical law of death *and* overcame that law at the same time. The magnitude of this single accomplishment is difficult to describe. The reason He was able to achieve such a great accomplishment —surrender His life for us—is because He was not concerned with worldly achievements. You see, even the closest disciples of Jesus wanted desperately for Him to chase worldly gain. They thought His worldly kingdom would be physically manifested here on Earth during their lifetime. His lack of worldly ambition even caused some disciples to fall away. Even His cousin, John the Baptist, displayed doubt because of Jesus' lack of concern for worldly conquest (Matthew 11:3). However, Jesus had a mission to set the entire world free, not just one generation.

Note that even this greatest of all human achievements is not a hill where we as His children can set up camp. Someday we will move past it into eternal life and fellowship with Him. However, the hill where Jesus bought our freedom on the cross is the only hill worth pointing back to during our short stay here on Earth.

Accomplishments can be exhilarating and meaningful in our walk through this life. However, it is important to keep a proper perspective and look at them in the context of what they truly represent. Accomplishments are hills among the valleys of our journey.

Each step you take in your journey through life, every hill you climb, each obstacle you overcome, and every test you pass is a significant check-point along your journey. These are significant and meaningful times in your life that build character, mold the person you are, and energize you to take on the next hill. I challenge you to keep each promotion, goal achievement, and each title you earn in the perspective of a Lego piece. Each achievement is a large building block in a much larger grand structure that is your entire life and who you are. So enjoy the exhilarating feeling of a great achievement for a time, then move on in your journey, keeping your eyes fixed on and your sense of worth deeply rooted in Christ.

5

CANNED IDENTITIES

WHOEVER SEEKS GOOD FINDS FAVOR, BUT EVIL COMES TO
ONE WHO SEARCHES FOR IT.
PROVERBS 11:27

Now that I've set the tone for what identity is and I've given some examples of the types of things many people see as their identity, we can move on to some practical steps and applications in real life.

Let me introduce a distinction between subjective and objective identity.

Subjective identities are things people (us or others) believe about us that we try to uphold. If we allow this to be our focus, we are allowing what others think about us to become our reality.

Objective identities are facts about who we are. These are things we cannot change.

When the two worlds of subjective and objective combine, others will attempt to impose identities on us based on objective realities. This is a dangerous place to be because it seems to be rooted in truth. Allow me to elaborate.

When someone places expectations on you based on who they think you should be, that is a subjective identity. Here's an example: Timmy, a nine-year-old boy, falls off his bicycle and bruises his arm. As the pain becomes a reality to him, tears pool in his eyes. He then feels his throat tighten and suddenly his body involuntarily begins to cry. His friends are not trying to be mean, but they urge Timmy not to cry. His father then comes out of the house to see what the commotion is. Upon seeing Timmy crying, the father urges Timmy to stop crying, picks him up, and takes him into the house. After Timmy has calmed down, his father uses this opportunity to teach a life lesson that every man has to learn. Men don't cry. The father may even layout plans and examples to illustrate his point. He will give tips on how to overcome the pain. Knowing that Timmy looks up to his best friend's 15-year-old brother, Sam, he asks, "Have you ever seen Sam cry?" When Tim replies that no, he hasn't seen him cry, his father presses the point: "That's because men don't cry."

Timmy's objective identity, being a male, has resulted in a subjective identity of how a male should respond to pain.

It may not be conveyed in such a direct manner, but at some point in each man's life, he will usually be presented with a similar "life lesson." He will then allow that subjective expectation of himself as a male to determine whether or not he will allow himself to cry. This illustrates how we can fall prey to assuming a subjective identity—one that someone has imposed on us. It's not something that we decide for ourselves; it's something that someone else decided concerning who we should be or how we should think or act, based on their expectations. When we accept a subjective identity, we fall into the trap of believing that identity defines who we are.

I like to call subjected identities "canned identities." When I buy a can of tomato soup in the store, I know exactly what I will get every time. The ingredients never differ, and the taste is always the same from one can to another. I can pick it up, look at the ingredients, and determine the nutritional value – or choose to ignore the nutritional ramifications for the sake of a yummy dinner.

This is often what we do when we meet someone. We look at their labels: appearance, style, how they speak, how they carry themselves, and more. Our mind immediately reaches deep into our subconscious for one of our cans on the shelf. If this new person appears similar to someone we had an experience with before, we place them in a can in our mind. That can encompass most of their attributes along with everyone else we perceive to have the same characteristics. This is based on their surface and labels we have immediate access to. This reaction is natural and normal. As long as you never go deeper than a surface relationship with that person, you will subconsciously set them on a shelf next to all the other cans of the same brand and ingredients.

In 2008, I was honorably discharged from the Marines. I then began making a life for myself as a civilian and got married shortly thereafter. To this day, I still meet people who are surprised when they learn that I was enlisted in the Marine Corps for five years. This, of course, happens primarily with people who were not in the Military. They are surprised because, on the surface, I don't match their "Marine" can. The Marines on their shelf may be loud, extroverted, and tough-looking. Because I tend to be quiet, introverted, and appear a little soft and gentle, it surprises many when they discover I was in the Marines.

Furthermore, I rarely bring up my military past in discussion. This further conflicts with their expectation that people who have spent time in the service always find a way to bring it up in conversation.

However, when they discover I was a Marine, what happens to their expectations of me? They then have two choices: they could try to fit me into their Marine can in their mind, or they can get to know someone unique. If they choose the latter, it may change the way they view Marines. But which scenario do you think is more probable in most cases?

Let me put it another way. Which is easier: attaching a label and moving on, or taking the time and making the emotional and cognitive investment to get to know someone on a deeper level?

It's helpful to be aware that this phenomenon is a natural response that allows our minds to conserve time and energy. The simple truth is that we don't need to get to know the majority of people we meet past a surface level. Therefore, our brains save us unnecessary expenditures of energy by putting people in cans on a shelf.

It becomes problematic when the labels on our cans are so broad and generic that our perceptions become skewed and we end up in bigotry. In other words, it becomes an issue when we try to fit an entire class of people into one can.

You will find that the subjective identities others assign to us are usually based on objective realities: facts that do not change. For instance, your physical features are objective. Your family of origin and the place where you were raised cannot change. You cannot go back and change an ugly mistake that happened in your past. These are objective realities. When speaking about the "canned identity," it is almost always based on objective realities. That is why it can be so difficult and problematic when we are expected to fit into the can someone else has designed for people like us. Their expectations may be based in truth, but that truth does not encompass the vast reality of who we are.

I'm now going to expose canned identities for what they are. When we impose a canned identity on someone, it is a simplistic and narrow view of that person. Let me state this again. When we place someone in a can, we are reducing them to a label we recognize so we can maintain a small view of that person.

Again, this is practical for surface interactions, e.g., a visit to a store or gas station. Therefore a small view in most interactions is essential to a peaceful life. However, it is quite problematic for anything relational.

This becomes especially problematic when you try to establish your identity based on the perceptions of others. If you are preoccupied with the way others see you, you will live a life of frustration. This is because it is impossible to live within the bounds of someone else's "can." Not because others' expectations are enormous, but because their expectations are so limited. They have reduced you to fit into a can on their shelf. They have relegated your being, the vastness of your soul, and who you are into 15 pre-packaged ingredients on a label with a header that reads "tomato soup."

But you are not tomato soup—even if you look like it on the surface. The whole of your being cannot be condensed into 15 ingredients.

That is why I say it is impossible for you to "live up" to another's expectations of you because, in the process, you would actually be "living *down*." This will cause endless frustration because you will never be able to contain the vastness of your emotions, experiences, styles, and beliefs into 15 ingredients. It is absolutely preposterous to try to fit yourself into the can someone else has designed for you.

Now take into consideration that thousands of other people each have a different can for you in their mind. In other words, there are thousands of versions of you living within the minds of thousands of people – this depends on their personal experience with you. This furthers the extent of the impossibility to live up – *or down* – to the expectations of others. Again, when you realize the futility of trying to fit the reality of who you are into cans others have designed for you, you can free yourself from the need to meet their expectations and match their perceptions.

As mentioned earlier, being too eager to slap a broad label on a can may lead to unnecessary bias and bigotry. I'll stop short of talking points about racism or other labels; it's clear that when you place someone in a can in your mind, based on their physical appearance, you run the risk of overgeneralizing a large segment of the population.

Furthermore, when a person is trying to leave past mistakes behind, their subjective identity will attempt to minimize them in their current condition. Imagine a man who does some jail time for a bad mistake in his past. He then finds Jesus during his incarceration. Renewed as a changed and reformed man, he then tries to reintegrate into society after being released. However, some of the people who knew him before he did time will still see him as the man he once was and continually remind him that he is an ex-convict. He may have a difficult time shaking that label and even escaping that "can" in his mind. This could hinder him from becoming all he was meant to become in life.

Again, this is a subjective expectation based on objective facts. Although we all must deal with the consequences of our past actions, our past actions do not have to define who we are. Furthermore, being a fact does not give past actions the right to rule your life.

The concept of canned identities is found everywhere throughout our lives. It is very difficult to escape the world's attempt to impose an expected norm upon you based on the facts of your situation.

I cringe every time I see a sign that portrays something like, "Firemen support John Jakes for mayor!"

Well, wait a minute!! Are firemen not people? Is the fire department not made up of individuals? How, then, can we subject an image onto a group of people, with an expectation that they must act in one accord based on their choice of career?

This is what the world tries to do to us on a daily basis. Particularly through the media. Every time you see a message that overgeneralizes a certain demographic based on external factors, I would challenge you to step back and ask yourself if they are canning individuals in that segment of the population.

Now that I've explained all of this, it may seem there is no benefit to be had from canned identities that we project on others. However, that is not the case. There are some benefits to this concept, and it is, in fact, necessary for a normal lifestyle.

First of all, a subjective identity can cause us to do the right thing. It would be nice to think we always did the right thing for the sake of right versus wrong, but that just isn't the case. Especially when the "wrong" side is a little vague because it comes in the form of not doing anything.

Imagine the following scenario as an example: Before heading out on his commute, Jason stops by the gas station to purchase his morning coffee and a snack. As he is leaving the building, he sees a man sitting on the sidewalk in worn clothing. The man gets his attention by speaking to him and extending his hand, clearly asking for money. Jason mumbles something, turns his back, quickly jumps into his car, and drives away. Now let's run this same scenario again in a different way. This time, Mark is carpooling with Jason. Mark is not a Christian and Jason has been attempting to gently lead him to the Lord by example and sharing small tidbits of the Gospel occasionally. This particular morning, Jason even mentioned generosity as an admirable trait. When Jason and Mark exit the gas station, they encounter the same man on the sidewalk asking for money. Knowing that Mark considers him to be a generous Christian man, Jason digs into his pocket and gives the man a couple of dollars. No doubt, Jason did a good thing. However, he did it because he knew that Mark expected him to act generously, based on Jason's label and the generosity he has proclaimed. This is just one example of how good things can come as a result of the expectations associated with subjective identities. However, it is best to do good things from a genuine place of freedom characterized by a desire to do good things, rather than out of a sense of obligation. In other words, it is better to do good as a manifestation of your identity rather than doing good to protect a proclaimed identity. Nonetheless, the results can still be good.

This same principle applies to so many areas of our lives. If others perceive us as a hard worker at our workplace, we make an extra effort to be productive, even when we don't feel like it, because we want to maintain that image. Maybe you know a leader at church who thinks of you as someone who is very generous with your time, so they ask you to do more than you really want to do. You comply with their wishes because you don't want to disappoint them or compromise their view of you in any way. This is the trap we can fall into, allowing even a good subjective identity to control our actions. But this is not a way to live our lives.

No matter how highly someone thinks of you in any connection, they could never have enough space in their brain to grasp the full reality of who you are. It is impossible to "live up" to someone's expectations of you. Again, this would mean you would have to try to "live down" to the limited view they have of you. This is not because they think poorly of you, but because nobody has the capacity to think highly enough of you to encompass the fullness of your mind and soul. It is simply impossible.

With this knowledge, it is important that we project good onto others. Although we cannot grasp the entirety of someone else's soul, we can choose to have good expectations of everyone. Children in particular need positive expectations projected onto them. For a significant portion of a child's life, they will inevitably form their identity around what their parents think of them. Therefore, it's important to plant positive seeds. The challenge comes when we must release any notion that our children fit into a can. We never want to limit their ingredients. Rather, subjective identities that open the child up to endless possibilities is the best way.

No matter who we interact with, I suggest keeping open cans on your shelves. Placing people inside the cans of your brain is a necessary way of life. We simply do not have the mental capacity nor the time to get to know every person we ever come into contact with. So placing people inside cans is essential to an organized brain. However, if your cans do not have a lid, you can easily move someone from one can to another or give them a shelf of their own. When we don't have the benefit of full knowledge of who a person is, it's important to keep a flexible mindset concerning the way we view others. This will help us to stop short of limiting their value. On that note, it is also very important to ensure we don't assign value to the cans, as everyone has equal value in God's eyes.

But what about you? Should your identity be subjective or objective? As a Christian, you must seek to find your objective identity in objective facts. Those facts about who you are can be found in The Word of God.

You are a child of God (Galatians 4:7).

You are righteous (Romans 5:1).

You are worthy (Colossians 1:10).

You are blameless (Philippians 2:15).

You are God's masterpiece (Ephesians 2:10).

When Jesus died for you on the cross, he bestowed upon you the right to act in these identities. You did nothing to achieve them – you did the opposite. However, that is the epitome of the good news that the apostles brought to the world. You have the right, paid for by the blood of Jesus, to claim your identity in Him and His works. With these true and factual identities planted in you, you inevitably will continue to seek ways to fulfill them in your actions.

Others may paste a label on you that is meant to define who you are. Your job is not to try to change their mind or force your way out of their can. Keep in mind they have reasons for the estimation they have made. However, you must walk in the truth that their belief of who you are can never fully encompass the amazing whole person that you are: mind, body, spirit, and soul. This removes the pressure on you to act according to their expectations and it also removes the need to justify yourself.

In closing, I challenge you to use this knowledge to be more understanding of others in two ways. First, understand and be aware that other people do not have the capacity to fully understand who you are. Therefore, you should never be offended by someone else's expectations of who you should be. Rejecting who they expect you to be is not the same as rejecting them. Don't allow bitterness to take root when someone else doesn't understand you. Next, be fully aware of the fact that your brain cannot encompass the fullness of who someone else is, which is why it is important to regard others with an "open can" mentality that allows them to grow in your mind. Furthermore, the knowledge that each person who comes into your life is a child of God who is designed for a specific purpose will allow you to assign them their true worth. It is not devaluing to place someone in a can in your mind, but you are devaluing them if you keep them there as you get to know them in a deeper way.

6

CONDITIONAL IDENTITIES

BY THE HUMILITY AND GENTLENESS OF CHRIST, I APPEAL TO YOU – I,
PAUL, WHO AM "TIMID" WHEN FACE TO FACE WITH YOU, BUT "BOLD"
TOWARD YOU WHEN AWAY!
2 CORINTHIANS 10:1

Conditional identities are those that change based on our surroundings and the people around us. Although a necessary part of life, conditional identities must be managed and understood.

Some of you may balk at the notion that your surroundings play a big part in who you are. You may also resist the idea that who you are can change in an instant in response to a change in your surroundings. However, as we explore this principle, keep an open mind and open heart to the truths I will present. Understanding this principle and properly managing it can lead to an emotionally healthy mind. It allows us to live in peace and make progress in assigning the correct order to our identity hierarchy. As I present this principle, you can decide if it is relevant to your life.

So who is affected by these identity crises? Only the weak-minded? Allow me to illustrate how everyone can and does succumb to various conditional identities – sometimes several times a day.

There was a time in my life when I worked as a real estate agent. In the early stages of my career, I would rise early in the morning, go to the office, meet with the broker and team members, print off some flyers, and head out to prospect for clients. (Yes, I was that guy knocking on your door saying, "Hi, I'm Michael Lewis with so-and-so real estate.") The script and plan to knock on doors took hours of preparation before ever going out. I needed to know what to say and try to anticipate any questions that might come. When I was trying to sell a service to strangers, my role as an expert representing a real estate company obligated me to appear to have the answers. If they asked a question I could not answer, I would promise to follow up. Expectations were attached to my position as an expert. Any lack of confidence would mean certain rejection. As you can imagine, rejection was already a big part of that process.

When I arrived back at my office early in my career, I spent a lot of time asking questions of my broker and learning from him. I had to be willing to learn various methods and strategies to build a successful business.

Later on that same day, after my real estate work was finished, I would go home. At home, I was a husband. As a husband, I have obligations to listen to my wife and care for her needs. I cannot approach her the same way I would approach a stranger with the expert persona. Furthermore, I don't approach her the same way I approach my broker, asking questions in 'learner mode.' That would be inappropriate when I'm at home, and probably very annoying to my wife, who is also my best friend. It would be ridiculous to treat her the same way I treated clients, coworkers, or managers.

And that is my point about conditional identities. These are the necessary adjustments we make throughout most days. As a normal part of life, this is not an idea we need to shun. Rather, we should embrace it and understand it so we can grow in the knowledge of why we do the things we do.

As we go through our days, we are inevitably faced with conditions that change from one hour to the next. Here are some more examples of conditions we face daily that can alter who we are or the way we present ourselves.

When I'm at home, I don't speak to my children in the same way that I talk to my wife. My expectations as a father differ from my expectations as a husband.

Depending on your line of work, your interaction with customers differs from your interaction with co-workers or managers.

On social media, you probably don't post the worst parts of your life. You post perfect pictures of your perfect family. It may not represent your full reality, but it is your social identity.

And now we get to the big one: church identities. When we arrive at church, there's the pressure to become spiritual on another level. We may speak differently, smile more, and play our part in maintaining a certain culture.

It may not sound good or be a pleasant thought, but we're talking about reality. We must come to grips with the fact that our surroundings affect the way we behave. It is not always a bad thing, and flexibility is a necessary part of life.

Having the ability to adapt your demeanor based on your surroundings is usually critical to the normal functions of life. There is a reason for wearing different hats throughout the day. You will do much better at your job and be a more efficient worker if you are not trying to approach it the same way you approach your toddler or teenager at home. Again, those different hats represent your different identities.

Having situational awareness of your surroundings can give you the freedom to grow in areas where rigidity would be a hindrance. There is freedom when you choose not to be reduced to only one hat in your wardrobe.

The reason this comes down to identity is because it highlights the person you must become to function properly in your surroundings. Your goals change when you get to work. Also, the expectations others have of you change, and you have an obligation to respond to those expectations. The ability to figuratively turn the switch on and off based on an understanding of your surroundings—and the various expectations associated with each setting—is a sign of emotional maturity.

For example, think of someone who is accustomed to being a domineering leader. If they believe their identity as a leader must be at the forefront at all times, they may be limiting their growth and learning potential. Why? Because, when you are trying to learn something new, it is important to put on your student hat.

Rigidly holding onto and protecting an identity when another would be better suited to the situation is a quick way to offend others and make yourself look like a fool.

Let's take a look at the other side of the coin. Although there is good reason to be flexible, there comes a point when too much flexibility or inappropriate changes in behavior can be a detriment. To properly use this knowledge, you must be fully aware of your situations and the expectations attached to each one. If you remain oblivious to situational changes, you will not understand why certain identity changes are occurring.

This, of course, is dangerous, because you will find yourself acting a certain way without understanding the reason. This lack of awareness will lead you to fight the changes your mind is naturally making to the outward expression of who you are based on your new situation. Therefore, you will not allow yourself to transition freely and appropriately between various identities for the sake of your current situation.

When you are not aware of changes in your surroundings, you may feel insecure, as if your identity is under attack. If you don't know why you are suddenly acting differently in a particular situation, a part of your brain comes alive, screaming a warning that something is wrong. This warning may feel uncomfortable. The feeling of insecurity inside you may make you question who you are. However, it is not really a problem. Rather, it is a signal to alert you that you may need to adjust to your surroundings.

Nevertheless, this is one of the dangers of wearing different hats. Insecurity is rooted in questioning your identity, and there is no quicker way to question your identity than by acting in a way you realize is inappropriate for a particular setting. This triggers thoughts like, "Why did I say that?" or, "Do I fit in here?" etc.

We've all experienced those emotions. They often emerge when we have not correctly detected an automatic shift in our surroundings, or we have not shifted our identity accordingly.

One setting where this can happen, causing you to question your identity, is when two of your worlds collide. For example, when your spouse meets your coworkers for the first time at a work party, he or she may meet a "new you" as well. This depends, in part, on the degree to which you feel the need to adjust your identity at work. This scenario can be disastrous if one or both of you do not understand the principle, and you're not aware of the need to change hats. Again, confusion and insecurity can set in. You've probably heard the lines, "I don't even know who you are when you're around that person," or "This is who I have to be at work." There is truth to these statements. However, without a full awareness of your surroundings, you may hurt someone you love if you do not properly account for expectations from both sides when your two worlds overlap.

We see some Biblical examples of this. Think back to when Jesus' mother and brothers came to visit Him while He was teaching and preaching (Mark 3:31-35). They sent someone through the crowds to tell Him they were there. What was His reply? "Who are my mother and my brothers?" Wow, can you imagine the hurt and pain this must have caused His family—and His mother in particular? They had come to visit Him, and He used it as an opportunity to teach a lesson to those around Him. Think about the implications of this action. Can you see the two worlds that came together in that instance? Jesus' mother and brothers knew Jesus as the son of Mary and Joseph. To them, He was a family member traveling the world doing speaking engagements. So if they did not adopt a proper awareness that He was in a teaching environment, they might take it pretty hard that He did not acknowledge their importance over those around Him. Furthermore, the fact that this passage made it into the Bible indicates it was a scandalous thing to say. At the very least, it certainly raised a few eyebrows.

Most of you have met people you know in more than one setting. For instance, you may see a colleague at church, or run into your boss at the grocery store. When this happens, you may notice that the same person you know so well in one context acts quite differently in another. If we have a proper understanding of these principles, we will not be offended and caught off guard when that person doesn't act according to our original expectations.

I'm not suggesting you treat your family members like second-class citizens when you are in your work environment. However, this story does illustrate the importance of being aware of the conditional identity a person adopts to adapt to a certain setting. Furthermore, if we are not careful to tune in to our conditional identities, we may act out of character in a given situation and hurt those we care about. A proper understanding of this principle can also help us avoid being offended when we encounter someone we know on a social level who may act differently when we encounter them in a professional environment – and vice versa.

Let's take a more in-depth look at the two extremes to our shifting identities. Both extremes are a hindrance to growth. First, we will look at strict rigidity, and then we'll consider the free-floating identity. You have likely found yourself in both of these categories at some point in your life's journey and you may find yourself operating daily in one now.

If you adopt a strict, rigid attitude, you may be tempted to think, "If they don't like who I am, it's their problem," or "They are just jealous or intimidated by me." This type of forefront identity will close you off to new opportunities and relationships that could lead down a path of further fulfillment. With this rigid attitude, such a person may well take the road towards isolation and loneliness.

When my wife and I were in our mid-twenties, we opened our first business: a dance studio. To our surprise, the friends we had in our age group often distanced themselves from us. Furthermore, when the friends we had brought together at the studio would gather outside the studio, they often excluded us. Of course, this hurt in the beginning. In response to this perceived affront, we adopted the following attitude: "They don't understand us, and they never will." Unfortunately, we took the route of rigidity rather than trying to understand why we were being excluded. We saw ourselves as business owners and reasoned that the others in our age group were not on the same path.

This is not a story of bitterness but of observation. My wife and I were operating without the understanding of conditional identities. Although we had assumed the new identity of being business-like in our interactions at the studio, we failed to recognize the difference in the interaction of our friends who were now our customers.

This led to isolation. Fortunately, my wife and I were together in our isolation, but isolated just the same. Sadly, isolation is at the root of many problems in life, and it can easily exacerbate our sins. In other words, isolation brings the worst parts of us to the surface. It was not until we removed that rigid "This is who we are" mentality that we began to live in freedom. We had done what we believed necessary to run a successful business. It did, of course, serve a purpose. However, the rigidity we had adopted initially had already done its damage and wounded many relationships, some of which could not be mended.

The other extreme of conditional identities is the free-floating identity. This is the person who is constantly pulled to-and-fro without the ability to control their emotions and actions. When you are operating in a free-floating identity, you will always feel like you are controlled by your surroundings. This points to a weak primary identity and is the most dangerous way to live. This type of fluctuation in identity will cause frustration, insecurity, fear, and exhaustion.

As I mentioned earlier, a lack of understanding and awareness as to why one is acting in a particular way is very frustrating. Furthermore, if you find yourself acting in a way that you don't anticipate, and you don't understand what is causing it, that goes beyond frustration – it's frightening!

If we are honest with ourselves, we have all experienced similar moments of identity crisis before. It can be part of the natural progression that occurs as we become independent people and build our character, bit by bit. Some seek more meaning and understanding when this happens, while others over-correct into rigidity. Some choose rigidity as their safety net; others choose a free-floating identity, which only breeds continual confusion. Both of these choices are dangerous.

Let's look at a Biblical example of someone who understood the concept of situational awareness and used conditional identities to his advantage.

In 1 Corinthians 9:22, Paul tells us, "To the weak, I became weak to win the weak. I have become all things to all people so that by all possible means I might save some." This is not a free-floating identity crisis Paul was dealing with. He had a specific goal in mind, and he knew exactly what he was doing. He embraced his identity as an apostle of Christ in the opening of each one of his letters. Nevertheless, knowing that he was also called to take the message to the Gentiles, he was well aware that he could not approach them with a pious attitude. Fortunately, God had made it clear to Paul that he was not obligated to conform to the traditional Jewish rules. He had granted him an extra measure of freedom from certain Jewish rules, and in some situations, he had to live in the freedom God had granted him.

Although he still chose to abide by those Jewish rules when appropriate, he also chose to live in freedom apart from those rules when it was necessary to reach people whose culture was not familiar with or bound by those rules. It must be noted that Paul did not set out to break the Jewish rules for the sake of freedom. In other words, he did not break the rules to show off that he was allowed to break them. When Paul was in the presence of other Jews, he conformed to the expectations of his peers and lived within the law (Acts 21:26). But the specific goal he kept in mind as he made these changes was to spread the Gospel of Christ.

You see, this is where people misunderstood and misjudged Paul then, and where they continue to misunderstand him today. He did not stand against the Jews, nor was he opposed to Jewish culture in any way. He simply had a proper understanding that the Jewish culture was not his savior; Jesus was. Therefore, when he departed from Jewish rules, it was not a matter of questioning his identity as a law-abiding Pharisee; rather, it was because he found his higher identity in

Christ. Christ had granted him the freedom to walk away from those rules when necessary to spread the Gospel.

The solution to the problems of rigidity and free-floating identities is simple, but it is not an easy concept to live out. Identity in Christ frees us from the bondage of conditional identity. Like Paul, on the one hand, it allows us to move between settings freely and securely wear different hats based on who we are with. On the other hand, it protects us from being pulled away from who we truly are in Christ. When we find identity in Christ, everything must first be filtered through our identity in Him.

You see, the root of a rigid identity is self-idolatry. Identity in Christ and knowledge of His awesome power in our lives will always destroy self-idolatry. Conversely, a free-floating identity signals the lack of personal identity; a close corollary is a constant seeking of the approval of others. When we find purpose and value in the identity Christ gives us, we have the tools to secure our personal identity and dispense with the need to seek others' approval. When we know who we are in Christ, we will not find our value in being rigid or in the acceptance of others. We no longer need their approval to discover who we were born to be.

7
IDENTITIES IN CONTROL

BUT YOU HAVE AN ANOINTING FROM THE HOLY ONE, AND
ALL OF YOU KNOW THE TRUTH.
1 JOHN 2:20

When God placed this message on my heart and told me to write a book about identity in Christ, I did not fully grasp the vastness of the subject. To be honest, I had not put much thought into the issue prior to this journey. However, immediately upon receiving the assignment to write this book, the Holy Spirit began to reveal to me the enormous subject it actually is. Furthermore, I began to see how almost every action we take and every decision we make comes down to our identity.

As humans, we like to believe we are in control at all times. At a minimum, we want to be in control of ourselves. That is why we balk at the notion that anyone or anything else has control over our actions. This desire for control is the reason so many Christians still struggle with their identities.

I'm submitting to you that it is near impossible to be fully in control of anything, including yourself. This is why it is so important to find your identity in Christ.

Our identity controls who we are, what we do, and the decisions we make. If we trust God to have our best interests in His heart, we can confidently surrender control and allow Him to lead us. Therefore, placing our top identity in Him keeps us safe because our actions will be a reflection of His leading on our lives.

If the previous chapters have not convinced you – or convicted you – about the controlling identities in your life or shed light on the subject, you may continue to struggle with this idea. Let me try to make it as plain as possible. Your identity is not defined only by the way you see yourself; it also reflects the way you believe *others* see you. In other words, you're simultaneously living up to your own expectations as well as the expectations you think others have of you. This could explain why you may occasionally do things you don't understand. Remember the salesperson who sold you more electronics or gadgets than we needed or intended to buy?

The need to live up to an identity that we have projected is real. It's almost as if we consider ourselves a liar if we do not act according to an identity that we are projecting to someone else. This attempt to protect our projected identity is usually an automatic reaction to our surroundings and usually goes undetected.

It seems such a small thing, but the effect it can have on your life is huge. Although you may want to dismiss the reality that you have various identities controlling what you do at different times, you really only need to look back on your life over the past few weeks. Consider some of the scenarios you have been in and the various ways you have acted in different settings. As you do, it's important to suspend any judgments you may have formed concerning the concept of having multiple identities. Once you embrace this concept as part of your truth, you will have the freedom to continue your life's journey with the understanding that you must prioritize your identity hierarchy. When you have a proper understanding of the role your identity plays in your life, you can consciously choose and operate in accordance with the appropriate characteristics, given each setting. This does not mean you are being weak-minded or that you are allowing yourself to be blown around like a leaf; it is the exact opposite. You do not lose strength by learning why you are doing things you don't want to be doing.

When our actions emerge from an identity that is not suited for our situation, people get hurt. Think back to the example when the spouse came along to the office party and was shocked to find out they were not married to who they thought they were. It's as if they were meeting that person for the first time—and not in a good way.

Think back on a time when you treated someone poorly, even though you loved them dearly. Then go back even further. Did your parents ever say some very hurtful things to you in their anger? Even if you were confident that they loved you, those hurtful things can travel with you and hurt you for years, and, in some cases, for a lifetime. Why would they do something out of character like that? Well, when we understand how identity works, we realize their actions reflected an identity crisis or a conflict. They loved you and wanted to be good parents. We have an expectation that good parents are kind. However, good parents have the expectation of being respected. When they feel disrespected, their identity as a respected parent is challenged. The frustration that comes with conflicting identities will cause anger to surface in some cases. Although this is not always the explanation, it exemplifies the importance of having an awareness of each of your identities.

For a Biblical example of identity gone wrong, let's look at a man after God's own heart. You might take a moment and read 2 Samuel chapter 11 for the full story. As the king of Israel anointed by God, David certainly had his share of great successes in the Bible. However, he is also remembered for one of his greatest moral failures.

While his troops were at war, King David took an evening stroll on his rooftop to get some fresh air. When he was looking out over his kingdom, something caught his eye. It was a woman taking a bath. Rather than turning away and running from sexual immorality, he indulged his lustful desires. David didn't even stop with simple lustful looks and thoughts. Taking it a step further, he asked his servants, "Who is that woman?" When they told him it was Bathsheba, Uriah's wife, David then sent his servants to bring her to him.

There can be only one explanation for David's intentions in sending for Bathsheba – and of course, he did proceed to commit adultery with her.

Let's stop here for a minute. What does this have to do with identity? Well, what kind of man would have the audacity to take another man's wife and sleep with her while her husband was at war? One possibility is that it was a man without a moral conscience. We know this was not the case with David, given the rest of his life story. This leaves us with another explanation: that David allowed one of his worldly identities to override his moral compass.

Which identity was controlling David's actions in this situation? It was his worldly identity as a king who had the power and authority to do as he pleased. Most men indulging in lustful thoughts from their rooftop would not have brought attention to this fact by asking others who she was. But David was a king, which made his actions unquestionable. Furthermore, imagine taking it a step further and asking them to bring her to him after being told she was Uriah's wife. His identity as a king who could not be questioned was in full control of his thoughts and actions throughout this story.

But then it got worse.

After David committed adultery with Bathsheba, he sent her home. Later, he found out she was pregnant with his child. David was on the verge of being discovered and exposed for his crime. So rather than stop and accept the consequences at that point, he tried to protect his reputation by sending for Uriah and getting him to sleep with Bathsheba so that Uriah would think he was the child's father.

Now, why did David take this a step further and try to cover up his sin by committing even more sin? Because he had a public image to protect. He had an image of being a strong and righteous moral leader and the king of his people. So he flip-flopped from the identity of "I can do what I want because I'm the king" to "I am viewed as a good king and moral leader." He was then being controlled by the image he had portrayed and what his people thought of him. Furthermore, in his desperation to protect his image, he took it as far as to commit murder to maintain an image.

This story of David and Bathsheba is a perfect example of how our identity, if mis-prioritized, can lead to some disastrous results and cause us to do things that seem outside of our character. Let's face this harsh truth: when David was doing these evil acts, he certainly was not acting from his identity as a follower of God. What does that say about you and me when we partake in sinful acts?

However, we should not despair about this, because there is a solution. Although we sometimes fall into bad habits or catch ourselves in prideful actions at times, if we give each of our controlling identities its proper place in the hierarchy of priorities, we will smooth out and lessen awkward and inappropriate interactions. Yes, in the coming chapters, I will cover more of our identity in Christ being the head of all our identities. However, a proper understanding of the lower leaders of our lives is important as well. It's important to note that God isn't asking us to have no other identity or responsibility outside of Him. Having an individually unique identity is not idolatry. However, having an identity above Christ most certainly is. Furthermore, identity in Him illuminates and strengthens the good qualities of our lives. Salt does not take away the tastiness of food; it enhances it. Light does not hide the various colors and unique features of a room; it makes them visible. When we are salt and light (Matthew 5:13-14), finding identity in Christ means we find true uniqueness and true freedom to be the children of God He created us to be.

A few years ago, I had a habitual struggle with immorality that had started at a younger age. Pornography and masturbation had a stronghold on me and refused to let go. When I tried to quit, I might have been able to go a month without it, but eventually, I would fall right back into it. This habit was in direct conflict with the person I was created to be as a child of God.

Furthermore, it conflicted with the image I portrayed as a good husband, church-goer, and a good father.

The spirit of lust is tricky. It told me to indulge because I deserved it. After all, lust said I had been working hard, my wife was mean to me, or I was missing out if I didn't partake. Furthermore, lust convinced me that I wasn't really doing anything wrong, and it wasn't hurting anyone. Of course, these were all lies designed to entice me to indulge in sexual immorality and self-idolatry.

The world said I was a man, assured me I had control of my own body, and therefore I had the right to do what I wanted. Nobody could tell me what to do. This, of course, is a warped view of a man's identity and what it means to be a man. It was not until I came to the point of truly seeking who I was meant to be that I gained freedom over this idolatry.

As a husband, I was a protector of my wife. When hiding the secret of pornography, I was a protector of pornography. As a father, I am supposed to be an example of a man led by God, offer my daughters security, and teach them discernment in finding a husband. When engaging in sexual immorality, I was acting in opposition to that identity as a good example. I had to recognize my priorities so that these identities were in conflict. And because they could not co-exist, I had to decide which was more important.

Make no mistake; sexual immorality cannot co-exist with your identity in Christ. Sexual immorality tells you it can be a part of your walk with God, but it most certainly cannot. I'm not going to get into whether you can be "saved" or not if you're stuck in pornography; that's not the point here. I am telling you it is in direct conflict with who you were meant to be as a follower of Christ. Furthermore, it's not even about the pornography per se. This is simply an example of how the correct priority in identities can pull us toward a righteous life – not away from it.

Placing my identity of husband and father over my selfish identity helped me gain freedom from a nasty and predatory slave master. Pornography tricked me into thinking I was acting in an identity of freedom. However, in reality, I was trapped; it was anything *but* freedom that I was living in.

The idea that we don't have control over our actions and we are led by our identities is not an easy one to process – you may even balk at the suggestion. We inherently like to believe we are in control of our own lives. To some extent, in the sense that we have free will to either follow God or follow the world, we are in control. However, when we follow worldly pleasures to fill our lives, we are not indeed free. We are free only when the Son sets us free. In Him is the only place we find true freedom. This is why it is so important to find identity in Christ. To have identity in Christ and to be led in His ways is so much better than being led by the ways of the world. If someone or something is going to be in control of your life, wouldn't it be best to have it be the Almighty Powerful God of the Heavens and Earth? Trust me; His ways are not only higher than ours, but His ways are also immensely better.

I will go further into some actionable steps to remove habitual sins from your life in a later chapter.

For now, I challenge you to recognize the areas in your life that are not aligned with your identity in Christ. Think of the sinful habits you may have a hard time shaking. Consciously bring these nasty habits that attempt to rule your life into conflict with your identity in Christ. Your highest identity in Him will give you the strength to live in true freedom.

8

INTERNAL CONFLICT

FOR THE FLESH DESIRES WHAT IS CONTRARY TO THE SPIRIT, AND THE SPIRIT
WHAT IS CONTRARY TO THE FLESH. THEY ARE IN CONFLICT WITH EACH OTHER,
SO THAT YOU ARE NOT TO DO WHATEVER YOU WANT.
– GALATIANS 5:17

Identities in conflict. How do we respond when one of our identities or defining characteristics is challenged? What do we do when tragedy strikes and our own strength, way of life, or beliefs come into question? How should we feel when a less than admirable trait surfaces in a stressful situation, even though we know we should behave differently?

Identities come into conflict when two or more of our worlds collide. It is important to understand the principles of identities in conflict so we can properly prioritize which one will take precedence in any given decision or action. This does not always constitute an identity crisis; we are designed to have identities coexist peacefully within us if we have carefully established a well-ordered hierarchy. Nevertheless, it is not uncommon to see our identities come into conflict. And when they do, it can influence us to act in ways that surprise us or push us to make short-sighted decisions. Allow me to elaborate further.

When I was a child, my family raised goats. This was a big part of our life. In a family of six, this placed a great deal of responsibility on us as children. At a very young age, my sisters and I had to feed, water, and milk the goats twice daily. Furthermore, our parents would allow us to take individual ownership of the goats when they were born. This meant the goats became our personal responsibility. As children, we became quite fond of certain goats, and we each had our favorites. When I was ten years old, I had a billy goat kid that I named Billy the Kid (yes, very original). He had a genetic defect that made it difficult for him to eat properly, so his health was compromised from birth. However, I invested my time in taking good care of him and made sure he got the milk he needed.

This went on for a while, but Billy the Kid's health issues finally caught up with him.

One morning my parents called me into their room and gently told me that Billy the Kid had died. I was so sad; I began to cry and sob for the loss of my little goat. Seeing this as a teaching opportunity, my father urged me not to cry, assuring me that death was simply a part of life. He didn't directly say this, but I took it as a lesson that men don't cry. After all, I had never seen my father cry. From that point forward, I internalized that crying was unacceptable. I learned to control that aspect of my life, contain my emotions, and resisted crying over "trivial" matters. For the rest of my life, I carried this lesson with me and fought the urge to cry at all costs.

Fast forward a few years (or decades).

A few years ago, I went through a bout of ill health. One morning, when I got up to start my day, my legs collapsed beneath me, and I flopped onto the floor like a bag of potatoes. It took all I had to crawl to the living room and call my wife to help me stand up. To my surprise, a pain that I had experienced in my left leg many years before returned without warning—with a vengeance! In the past, this pain had been isolated to my left leg. However, this time, it seemed to be connected to my lower back. I'm generally the type of guy who doesn't go to the doctor or take pain killers. Most pain will go away if you just wait long enough, right?

When I told my chiropractor about the pain, she mentioned that it might be sciatic nerve pain. My family doctor scheduled an x-ray and an MRI. When the results of my MRI came back, she seemed surprised by the severity of the condition. The pain was caused by a shift in my L5 vertebrae that caused a disk to bulge and come into contact with the sciatic nerve. She then referred me to a spine specialist who would recommend the correct treatment. However, before the appointment was over, my family doctor mentioned that I might need surgery at some point and that the issue was probably one I would have to manage for the rest of my life.

During the drive home, my head was spinning. My mind was a mess, and I couldn't think straight. Before I knew what was happening, I was panicking. This couldn't be happening to me. I felt myself getting emotional. But this wasn't a normal emotion; this was one I had long since banished to the depths of my heart. My wife was with me, and our two little girls were in the back seat, so I desperately tried to push these emotions back down. When I could no longer deny it, I suddenly had to pull over. This little unwelcome feeling was bursting to the surface, and I couldn't stop it anymore! I broke down and started to cry in front of my wife and small daughters. It took several minutes to pull myself together. Completely embarrassed, I drove home, confused and unhappy with myself.

How could I have allowed myself to break down and cry in front of my wife and daughters? After all, men don't cry.

This didn't make sense to me. Why was I so affected—to the point of crying? I hadn't cried in years. I had dealt with health issues before, so why was this different? I told myself others faced much worse situations every day without falling apart and dissolving in a puddle of tears. As you are reading this, perhaps you are experiencing something much worse than what I had to go through that day. I honestly didn't understand why I had this reaction until God took me on this journey, exploring the depths of identity and the immense roles they play in our lives.

The truth of the matter is, that situation challenged one of my identities and proved it to be insufficient. I am athletic, I love playing sports when I can, and I lift weights almost every day. At least I did before this happened. When I learned that I might have to go through back surgery and might well have to deal with the ramifications for a long time, my identity as an athletic person with a healthy body was severely wounded. Just contemplating the possibility that I might lose that aspect of my life threw a spotlight on the importance I had attached to that identity and exposed my fear of losing it.

Of course, there were other aspects to the larger situation, such as the prospect of not being able to play with my girls without limitations. But let me camp out on this one point for a bit.

We all have various identities or characteristics that define who we are. When these identities come into conflict with one another, when they are challenged or when they prove to be insufficient, it can cause us to do things we wouldn't normally do. This is based on the weight or importance you have attached to that identity in your life. In a surprising twist, these times of trial can produce a new identity in us. For instance, in the story about losing Billy the Kid, my deep sense of loss produced a new identity in me. After this loss and the decision I made in response to it, I adopted the identity of a man who does not cry. Later in life, when my identity as a physically fit and healthy man felt threatened, the thought of losing that identity was so overwhelming, it overrode my identity as a man who never cried. This exemplifies how significant events in our lives can cause two identities to come into conflict.

I hope you can understand the point here. Throughout our lives, there will be times when our identities or defining characteristics will be challenged, lost, or even come into direct conflict with one another. When this happens, it may cause us to do things we would not normally do. Can you think of a time when one of your identities was challenged, lost, or when it proved insufficient? If the instance you are thinking of involved an identity to which you attached a great deal of importance for years, you know it hurts. It may have caused embarrassment, insecurity, or even self-loathing.

When identities come into conflict, we can be tempted to feel insecure, insufficient, and vulnerable. However, let me assure you that these conflicts are simply a natural part of life. Even the strongest person you can think of has experienced conflicts between two or more identities in their life.

But you don't have to take my word for it.

Now I'm going to share a time when the greatest man to ever walk the earth faced an identity conflict—none other than Jesus Christ! Furthermore, this moment is defined in the shortest verse of the Bible.

Stay with me for a moment as I go through this. Try to read it with an open mind.

This example is based on John 11:35, "Jesus wept."

Why did He weep? Because He had just heard the news that Lazarus, His good friend, had died. But if you read the passage closely, you'll see that He had already broken the news to His disciples in verse 11 that Lazarus was dead—something He knew by divine knowledge. Furthermore, Jesus told them that He would raise Lazarus from the dead. This all happened prior to Jesus receiving the news from the Jews that Lazarus was dead, and prior to Him responding by weeping. Why would Jesus cry over the news that His friend had died when 1) He already knew Lazarus was dead, and 2) He knew He was about to raise him back to life?

I'm sure countless people have asked and answered this question through the years. However, I would like to present one possible answer I haven't heard of prior to this revelation.

I suggest that, although Jesus was divinely directed and He knew what was about to happen, He still identified with His human side in that moment of sadness. Jesus was fully God AND fully man. This means He had human problems, temptations, trials, and emotions. Jesus was subjected to all the same sadness, loss, and death we are subjected to today. It was necessary for Him to identify with His human side at times like this to fully grasp the meaning of being human. After all, life is filled with loss and sadness, so how could it be said Jesus dealt with everything we must experience if He did not also experience these earthly emotions? In that instant, it appears that two aspects of His identity were in conflict. On one hand, he had all-knowing divine power and knowledge. On the other, He was a man like us, and He had just lost his friend. Furthermore, as Lazarus's friend, the others with him who were mourning his death would have thought it very cold and callous to be blank-faced upon hearing this news. Therefore, He also had an identity to uphold, from an external perspective, as Lazarus's friend.

Am I suggesting Jesus was concerned with the views and thoughts of other people around Him?

Perhaps He was.

Perhaps there's more to the meaning of this action. In fact, there may be more to the meaning of many of His actions than immediately meets the eye. God knows everything. And Jesus is fully God. However, Jesus was also fully man. This is one of the main foundations of our Christian beliefs. Therefore, Jesus did not have the luxury of acting as God all the time. He was here on earth – by choice – to identify with humans and save us. Hebrews 4:14 says, "We do not have a high priest who is unable to empathize with our weaknesses."

We have an advocate in Heaven who can relate to EVERY human emotion we encounter. Jesus was here – He was fully man – and He lived a perfect life to pay for our sins. Along the way, He lived through pain, sadness, loss, hunger, anger, deception, betrayal, gossip, slander, excitement, fun, adventure, love, discrimination, hate... and yes, identity conflict.

These are things we all experience during our lifetime—indeed, there is no escaping these emotions!

Therefore, I suppose what I'm trying to say is Jesus did not always act as God in every situation. If He only identified as God, how could He then say He empathized with our human weaknesses? He had to experience these emotions as a human in order to relate fully and fulfill His purpose. He had to identify as a human.

Therefore, He identified as a human, even when He knew the outcome.

Yes, I am suggesting Jesus had an obligation to live in that identity where He would be concerned with what others thought of Him. This most certainly was not a high priority for Him, but I believe there is evidence of this throughout the Gospels.

Your identities can pull you in different directions. When they come into conflict with one another, one will take precedence. However, Jesus has demonstrated that it is not always the greater of your identities that comes to the surface. It's normal and natural to not always feel led by your highest identity. However, if you are born again, you know we have the assurance of victory in the end.

However, I feel the need to say that a conflict between identities is not always a crisis. Various identities coexist at any given time; those identities will inevitably come into conflict with one another at some point. Yes, a less than admirable identity may surface at times, but often the reaction that ensues is the appropriate one.

Identities come into conflict throughout our lives. Again, this is normal. If we can recognize the conflicts when they occur, we can learn to weigh what is happening and address the situation with a clear head. We may not like our emotional response, but we don't have to feel insecure if we understand what is happening.

When we place our highest identity in Christ, we can be secure in His leading. Other actions that are not spurred by our identity in Christ can surface, but on the other hand, they will not conflict with it, either. Furthermore, if I can digress very briefly, the reason it was so devastating when I thought I was losing my identity as an athletic person was because it was taken away so suddenly. This exemplifies the importance of not attaching too much importance to identities that can crumble and be taken away so quickly.

Identity in Christ and finding our value in Him can never be taken away. Therefore, identity in Him is the only identity that is safe from challenge or loss and it will never prove insufficient. This is why identity in Christ is so important. There is no other identity that can keep us safe and secure in any circumstance. That top hierarchal position of our identity structure must be reserved for the King of Kings, Jesus Christ. Anything else can crumble in an instant.

9

IDENTITY MANIPULATION

FOR SUCH PEOPLE ARE NOT SERVING OUR LORD CHRIST, BUT THEIR
OWN APPETITES. BY SMOOTH TALK AND FLATTERY THEY DECEIVE
THE MINDS OF NAÏVE PEOPLE.
ROMANS 16:18

"Ring, Ring."

"Dance studio, this is Michael, how can I help you?"
This story takes us back to when my wife and I owned a
dance studio in Hemet, California.

"Hello, I'm looking for classes for my daughter,"
says the lady on the other end.

"Great! how old is she?" I respond enthusiastically.
I then take her down the path of explaining the sched-
ule, the services we offer, the age and skill ranges of certain classes, and the whole pitch.

At some point, we reach the question of cost. I can't
tell you how many times it would go something like
this:

"How much does it cost?" After presenting the
price for the class she had chosen, I would hear a short
pause, followed by the inevitable question.

"Is this a Christian dance studio?" she would ask
with an expectant tone.

I would respond by explaining that we are Christians running a dance studio, so many aspects of our life come into how we run the business, but we do not label it a Christian business.

Then came the question, "But you charge for classes? I'm a Christian too, can my daughter come for free, like a scholarship or something?"

Now, if you're a person who pays for the services you receive without asking too many questions, this scenario may sound absurd to you. Perhaps you think this story seems unlikely. However, I can assure you, after running a dance studio with a Christian theme for six years, this type of exchange occurred on a weekly basis.

Why would someone assume the Christian label means they get free classes? Let me explain the dynamic at play here so we can understand why people act in this manner.

We've already established the control our identities have over us in the preceding chapters. You have begun to see how our identities cause us to act in predictable ways at certain times, while at other times, they move us to do things we don't understand. This is further complicated by the fact that, as humans, we feel a need to live up to the identities we have portrayed to others.

If we're not aware of these factors, it will be hard to remain vigilant when others try to use our identity to control or manipulate what we do. Whether they are doing this consciously or not is beside the point. This dynamic is at play in most emotionally-based arguments. When the other person launches an emotional plea, they are appealing to your identity as a caring person, a nice person, etc. Using identities to tug at our heart-strings is not always a bad thing, as long as we stay alert to what the other person is doing. Let's walk through this.

In the example I gave earlier, what was the person on the phone trying to do? She was appealing to my identity as a Christian to request some sort of discount or special treatment. If that were my only identity— or even my highest identity—in that scenario, I might have acquiesced to her request. She had a well-defined expectation of what it meant to be a Christian.

An attempt to manipulate through identity will almost always be preceded by linking the appeal to an admirable identity the other person values highly. It is an attempt to push the other person into a box with boundaries that are understood or accepted.

She was attempting to manipulate my view of Christianity to control an outcome that would benefit her. Think about it. This expectation was not based on *her* Christianity; she was trying to get the discount based on *my* Christianity. If it had been based on her Christianity, she would go anywhere and expect a discount because she was a Christian. I'm fairly certain she wasn't in the habit of going to the local grocery store and asking for a discount at the checkout based on the fact that she was a Christian. Therefore, the conclusion is she was trying to get the discount based on the fact that *I* was a Christian. Therefore, she was imposing an expectation of how I should act as a Christian.

This exemplifies how often we can fall into the trap of placing expectations on others based on who we think they are.

It is important to have a proper understanding of how this paradigm of identity controls what we do. Until we understand this dynamic, others will attempt to use it to manipulate us in certain situations. When people try to project their definition of who we are and impose certain expectations on us based on that projection, manipulation can occur.

At this point, you may begin to see how often this happens.

The entire world of marketing is driven by appeals to our identity. "If you're fashionable, fashionable people wear this." "If you're cool, cool people buy this new phone." "If you're classy, classy people drink this wine."

The list goes on and on. When it comes to salesmanship, marketing is almost always an appeal to identity. Furthermore, marketing always tries to tell us what someone like us is supposed to buy. "Do you care about the safety of your home? Then you need this home security system." These appeals attempt to link the things "we need" to who we think we are.

Politics is the arena where we see one of the clearest examples of how our identity is used to manipulate us. If you're Republican, you're supposed to have this specific set of ideals. If you're a Democrat, you're supposed to have the opposite set of ideals.

Remember canned identities? The major flaw with this two-party system is that it attempts to place everyone into one of two cans. This is impossible and absurd as we are all individuals. For example, your beliefs on abortion in no way dictate your beliefs on gun control. Your beliefs on homosexual marriage do not dictate your beliefs on immigration. These are completely separate issues. The two-party system in American politics places expectations on our belief system based on the political party with which we associate. It promotes the idea that each party has a pre-packaged set of beliefs that characterize every person who identifies with that party. In so doing, it has tricked many people into believing the country is divided down the middle. This is not an indictment of the political system; it's simply an assessment of how expectations can be imposed on us based on our identity. We must recognize that our individuality and our decisions and support cannot be canned into one of two positions.

Political alignment tries to tell us we are one of two types of soup. If I open a can of tomato soup, only tomato soup will come out. The contents of a sealed can cannot change their ingredients, and they cannot remove the label someone has placed on the can.

American politics even takes this a step further, telling us which party we belong in based on our career, upbringing, religious beliefs, or ethnicity.

When you have an awareness of these principles, you can recognize attempts to manipulate you through your identity. Identity manipulation most often comes in the form of an emotional appeal. Disguised as a call to live up to who you are—or who you project yourself to be—in reality, it is a call to live up to someone *else's* expectation of who you are or who *they* want you to be.

The lady's request for a discount on dance classes was a thinly veiled attempt to appeal to my identity based on the way she thinks Christians should run their businesses. She assumes that if I'm really a Christian, I will want to help other Christians, right? Well, yes, of course, I want to help other Christians, but the topic of discussion is not helping other Christians, it is a matter of business. Furthermore, I cannot operate in her definition of my identity. In that particular setting, I see myself as someone who has established a system for running a successful business. This means that I stick to my own rules, I'm responsible in my business, and I pay my bills on time. I equate those characteristics with following Christ as a responsible human being, setting a good example, and supporting my family. My identity as a responsible business person does not allow me to give discounts.

I cannot allow someone else to define my identity because they are incapable of holding the entirety of who I am in their mind. (In the same way that I am incapable of knowing the entirety of who they are.)

Still, we see these emotional arguments all the time. For example, "If you care about children, you should donate to this cause." If you accept that as the definition of caring about children, then your donation is the proof as to whether you really care or not. The message appeals to your emotions as well as to your identity as a caring person.

After all, doesn't any caring person want to help children?

This type of marketing uses a manipulative appeal to control your emotions, your actions, and your identity. It asks you to question your identity as a caring person if you do not donate. When faced with such a message, it's important to adopt a proper perspective. The general truth is that someone who donates to such a cause does so because they are a caring person. However, giving to the cause does not *make* them a caring person. Conversely, your choice not to donate does not mean you are not a caring person. This marketing paradigm is all backward. Your identity is not defined by your actions; your actions are a byproduct of your identity.

Furthermore, this kind of message is an attempt to appeal to one identity you have that seems good and neglect all the other responsibilities you have. You need to be responsible with your time and resources. Therefore, you cannot go chasing after every appeal made to your identity, even when rejection of offers to prove your goodness portrays you to be less than a good person. This is the importance of understanding who you are and being firmly rooted in your top identity in Christ.

It is not a bad thing to be aware of others' expectations. The actions they request of us are not usually bad in and of themselves. However, it is dangerous to allow others to place expectations on us based on who they want us to be. Based on a few defining characteristics they have detected in you, they have determined how they expect you to act. This imposes a standard we are to live up to. As we saw in the chapter on canned identities, it is impossible to live "up" to someone else's expectation, because their perception of you cannot fully encompass the entirety of your soul and who you are. The fullness of who you are cannot be contained in the small can of a few defining characteristics. Again, trying to "live up" to someone's expectations is actually "living down" to another's definition of what it means to be you.

Now that I've explained all this, it may appear to be all bad. However, there are times when allowing our identities to control what we do can be a positive thing. Furthermore, we can use the "manipulation" to our advantage. Not to be manipulative, but to attain certain goals. You can use your identity as a healthy person to help you say no to a piece of cake. You can appeal to your identity as a loving parent to refrain from yelling at your children. These are ways to help you appeal to your identity to achieve a goal.

However, it's important to remember that the goal or outcome is not what defines your identity. Not eating cake doesn't make you a healthy person; being a healthy person influenced you not to eat the cake. It may seem an insignificant statement, but the weight of this paradigm can change your outlook. Evaluating your actions to determine your identity is a very frustrating place to live.

Let's take a look at Acts 22:22-29, where Paul was arrested for preaching the truth and sharing his testimony. In this passage, he appeals to the Roman commander's identity to gain fair treatment. When the crowd tried to seize him, the Roman guards arrested him. Their plan was then to beat him with a whip. However, Paul escaped this beating by appealing to the Roman leader based on Paul's status as a Roman citizen. This citizenship – or identity – granted him protection and the promise of fair treatment. Furthermore, the Roman commander was obliged to conform to the rules. In this scenario, Paul used the commander's identity as one who follows the rules to evade a dangerous and painful situation.

However, I want to bring us back to the premise of this chapter. The main point here is the importance of not allowing others' expectations to determine your behaviors. You cannot allow their opinion of who they think you are, whether good or bad, to determine your choices and behaviors. This in no way diminishes the standard you are to uphold as a follower of Christ; rather, it expands upon it. You are not limited to the small view others insist on projecting onto you. If you find yourself captive to what others think of you and continually try to live down to their view – or definition

– of your identity, you are opting into a life of frustration. That's bondage!

This is why so many Christians live their lives feeling like they are in confinement. They see rules as restrictions holding them back from doing fun things. This is the epitome of legalism: thinking that following the rules makes you a Christian, rather than the other way around.

Let's bring this back full circle to the greatest man who ever lived. When Satan tempted Jesus in the wilderness, he presented two temptations with this condition: "If you are the Son of God..." (Matthew 4:1-11). Do you see the appeal to identity? Furthermore, this is not appealing to *any* identity; it is appealing to His *highest* identity.

Keep the following in mind; In conversation, the words "if you are" are the beginning of an appeal to your identity. The *identity* they appeal to may be true, but their *definition* may not be aligned with yours. Again, we're seeing the, "if you are... then do this," appeal. Their "if you are" may be true, but their "then do this" may not. Their definition of who you are—and the expectations they place on you relative to their understanding of that identity—are not necessarily true definitions and legitimate expectations.

The only One who has the authority to tell you who you are and what your identity means is the Most High God. Even when someone appeals to your highest identity, their definition of your identity should not control what you do with your life. God has not asked everyone to do the same thing and He has allowed everyone to have different interpretations and fulfillments of similar identities. My fulfillment of my identity in Christ will not look the same as yours.

For this reason, I implore you to learn to recognize those times when someone appeals to one of your primary identities in an attempt to gain an advantage. Live in the freedom that your identity in Christ affords, and don't allow others to manipulate your actions based on their small view of who you are as a child of God. Your worth is not found in conforming to their definition of who you are; it is found in accepting who God has already said you are.

10

AND DO THIS, UNDERSTANDING THE PRESENT TIME: THE HOUR HAS
ALREADY COME FOR YOU TO WAKE UP FROM YOUR SLUMBER, BECAUSE
OUR SALVATION IS NEARER NOW THAN WHEN WE FIRST BELIEVED.
ROMANS 13:11

A lack of identity. What picture does that bring to your head? You may think of a teenager trying different things to fit in. He appears to have no clue as to what he wants to do when he graduates from high school. Perhaps you had a similar experience during those years—you did not know what you wanted to do with your life, or you were afraid of what might happen when the time came to move out of your parents' home. Or maybe you imagine a young adult who hasn't started college, they appear to have no direction, and they don't seem to have much going for them. These are examples of a lack of identity with external signs. However, lacking identity goes deeper than that.

A lack of identity occurs with the loss of an external identity or the realization that your current top identity will come to an end. You can be very successful in worldly terms and still not have a clear understanding of your identity. Furthermore, the more one becomes successful by the world's standards, the harder it can be to find identity in Christ. The external success of a person does not in any way correlate with their identity in Christ or any primary identity of their own.

When I was in high school, various identities vied for control in my life. I played sports, so that was one aspect of my identity. However, because I did not have the athletic talent to go beyond high school, that was an identity that would end with graduation. In my senior year, I signed up for the delayed entry program of the United States Marine Corps, which means I would go to boot camp after I graduated from high school. This gave me a new identity. I was going to be a Marine. I started to feel superior to those who had no idea what they were going to do after graduation. After all, I was the only one out of my graduating class of 62 people who was joining the Marine Corps. It was quite the point of pride, I suppose. I had purpose. Nobody could question that direction of my life. However, just like the sports in high school, this, too, was an occupation that would only carry me so far.

When your top identity is centered on career achievement, you will always be searching for something bigger.

As I came towards the end of my time in the Marine Corps, the inevitable question came: What's next?

I started working in the casinos as a blackjack dealer immediately following my time in the Marine Corps. This was a step up in my mind because I was then earning more money than I had ever earned before. Unfortunately, this started me down a path of chasing higher salaries. In the meantime, God was already impressing upon me that something was wrong. As I looked down the path of what could be my future,

I knew there was something else I was meant for. I did not know what it was, but I did know that continuing in my current direction was not the way to get there. Therefore, even when I was offered a promotion in the casino, I declined because I knew that would take me a step further down the wrong road. This realization caused me to mentally distance myself from my external trajectory.

In this state of confusion during my casino career, I lacked a top identity in my life. I didn't know who I was meant to be, but I was confident I was on the right path towards finding it. In the previous chapters, we've covered how our behaviors emerge from different identities. However, generally speaking, we filter most of our thoughts, actions, and decisions through our top identity.

When a person lacks a leading identity, they search for something to attach themselves to. This could be accomplishments, a title, fitness goals, or the next step in one's education. They will attempt to reach for external things for validation. Sadly, many Christians find themselves in this state – right alongside me.

I was raised in a Christian home. Although being a Christian had always been a part of my identity, I hadn't yet fully allowed myself to have an actual identity in Christ. There's a difference.

We must put God first, acknowledge Him as our top identity, and filter all the others through Him. Otherwise, our world and emotions can get pulled any which way. The reason we get pulled in various directions when our identity is not rooted in Christ is because everything in this world changes, fluctuates, and can be taken from us.

For instance, if my top identity is found in my job, and I lose my job, that will go beyond the loss of a job; it will also be the loss of my identity. If you place your primary identity in your role as a spouse, you may sink into frustration and insecurity every time your spouse is unhappy with you. And if you lose your spouse, you will question your identity and risk losing that identity altogether.

A lack of primary identity is not always the product of having no direction. Sometimes along our life walk, we discover we have been on the wrong path, as I did in my casino job.

When I realized that I was on a path that had the wrong future for me, my identity came into question.

When you realize you're walking the wrong path, the struggle is wondering whether or not to turn back. The thought of starting over will usually make you feel as if you've wasted a lot of time on the wrong road. Nobody likes to feel like the last year, five years, ten years, or even more was a waste of time. But if you resist the decision to turn back, thinking it would be a waste of time, you can be sure you will continue moving further down the wrong trajectory.

Is there commitment you need to end or something you're doing that takes more time than it's worth? Have you invested so much time in it that it would feel like a waste to throw it all away? If you feel that way about something in your life, I want to help you remove that limiting belief right now.

The reassuring truth is, finding your identity in Christ is never starting over; it's always a step up.

You do not have to trudge back down the horizontal path back to the beginning of your journey. When you realize that your value and worth are in Him—not your position or your job—you will immediately be elevated.

Let me say this again in a different way because this is a really good revelation and someone reading this needs these words right now.

If you are walking down a road that you know you're not meant to be on, you do not have to go back to the beginning and start over. Once you start to focus on Him, you will never go backward; you will only go up. You will immediately be transported onto a higher road. This does not mean your external circumstances won't change for the worse at times, but your identity will no longer be anchored in those external circumstances.

When I was seven years old, my friends and I would start playing Life, the board game. I say "start" because we never finished. It was such a long game, and frankly not interesting enough to keep a few seven-year-olds' attention. We wanted to finish the game, but we had no reason except for the pride we would feel when we finished. When that motivation wore off, we would always end up tossing Life aside and playing something more exciting – and faster – like Wahoo. When we started playing Wahoo, we instantly felt better, had more fun, and got to finish a game.

Identity in Christ completely changes the game you're playing. It's as if you were playing a boring board game that seems to have no end, and you decide to quit mid-game so you can begin a new game, confident that it will be more fun. You don't have to turn around and retrace all the steps you took in the boring game to get back to the beginning then start over with the new. That's ridiculous! You just push the old game to the side and start playing the new game—and start having a good time!

That is what it's like when you change your mindset and start truly submitting and following Christ fully. It's a new and better game. There's no turning back down the same path that brought you here; no moving backward in life. When begin playing Christ's game, you are immediately transported to a higher way of living. You are given a new purpose—the highest purpose possible!

You've probably heard it said in Christian circles that everyone has a God-hole in their life or their heart. The idea is that until we fill that empty space with Jesus Christ, we will forever sense an emptiness in our soul. At some point, most people will try to fill that emptiness with other things: accomplishment, title, education, relationships, activities, etc. However, none of these things can take the place in our heart that was designed for our Creator. A God-hole that remains unfilled is an identity in Him that remains unrealized. Until our primary identity is anchored in Him, that space will remain empty or be only partially filled.

You see, it is possible to partially fill that God-hole when you have a lesser identity in Him. In other words, if you find your primary identity in your career and your identity in Christ is secondary to that, you will only have partially filled that space.

As long as your identity in Christ is secondary to anything else, you will never realize the true joy of following Him.

Another aspect of the Christian life is the servant's heart. A true servant's heart can come from nothing other than identity in Christ. Yes, you can be a servant apart from an identity in Christ, but you cannot have an identity in Christ and not have a servant's heart. A servant's heart does not mean constantly serving; it means constantly understanding your value as well as the value of everyone else based on who Christ says you are. You cannot be secure in service if you don't know your true value as defined by God. I will cover this more in detail in a coming chapter.

When we lack identity, we do not realize who we really are in Him. Regardless of the external circumstances in life, we can always find our identity in Christ. A true identity in Christ does not hinge on our current situation as a definition of who we are. Those external factors are simply things that happen in our lives, the consequences of our actions, and rewards for being good stewards. Our circumstances can change on a whim, but our identity in Christ must be firmly planted.

Your identity in Christ will keep you looking up to Him through the hills and the valleys. You can find value in anything of this world, but no identity can elevate you higher than a primary identity in Christ. The freedom granted you through identity in Him will always be a step up.

I challenge you, whatever season of life you're in, take a quick evaluation of your current state of mind and circumstances. Are you currently allowing your identity in Christ to fully guide your thoughts and decisions? Are you holding on to anything from your past, or staying in a job you know isn't the right path for you, or living in a town you don't feel safe in, or keeping a relationship in your life, thinking that if you left, it would feel like you had wasted the past few years?

If any of these scenarios resonate with you, or any other situation in your life fits the principles found in this chapter, I challenge you to look up to God and ask for His true direction. Take a step of faith and step up to the higher path. *Start playing the new game now!*

If you're on the wrong path today, it will still be the wrong path tomorrow, next week, and five years from now.

At some point, you have to turn it all over to Christ and follow Him if you are to find your true worth and value as defined by Him.

11

THE ALTAR OF ADDICTION

YOU MUST NOT MAKE FOR YOURSELF AN IDOL OF ANY KIND OR AN IMAGE
OF ANYTHING IN THE HEAVENS OR ON THE EARTH OR IN THE SEA.
EXODUS 20:4

As a young child who grew up in a Christian home, I heard many Bible stories containing idols and altars. I was baffled by Aaron building a golden calf for the Israelites to worship. I remember hearing and seeing pictures portraying how Elijah mocked the prophets of Baal who danced around their altar and cut themselves trying to get their god's attention. When I was about ten years old, I saw a woman wearing a necklace with a little fat man sitting cross-legged. I asked my mother what it was; she told me it was an idol. At that age, it was a little eerie to come in such proximity to an idol in real life. Also, having read and heard the terrible stories of idols in the Old Testament, it was astonishing to think people still had them today.

We often think of idolatry as this ancient thing. We picture people building golden images and bowing down to some inanimate statue that cannot do anything for them. Most of us would laugh at the idea of creating something with our hands and openly proclaiming that to be our god. In American culture, this idea of idolatry makes it a little too easy for us to dismiss what idolatry really is. Idolatry is no laughing matter!

To try to capture the significance of it, let's redefine the term. Idolatry is not confined to bowing down and openly worshiping a golden calf; rather, we engage in idolatry each time we place anything above Christ.

What does this have to do with identity? Well, based on the definition I use in this book and the practical side of identity, you can see that we operate in multiple identities and roles as our values shift and change in response to our surroundings, our ambitions, and other factors.

However, the danger comes when your top identity is found in anything outside of Christ. Finding your value and worth in anything above your identity in Christ is idolatry. The keyword here is *above*. It's not wrong to pursue accomplishments in this world, but it is idolatry to find your value in them.

Placing anything above Christ is idolatry. Being *led* by anything other than Christ is idolatry. You cannot have Christ as your primary identity and allow other things to rule your life.

NO ONE CAN SERVE TWO MASTERS, FOR EITHER HE WILL HATE THE ONE
AND LOVE THE OTHER, OR HE WILL BE DEVOTED TO THE ONE
AND DESPISE THE OTHER. YOU CANNOT SERVE GOD AND MONEY.
MATTHEW 6:24

This is a hard truth, but I want it to instill hope in freedom through Christ rather than condemnation. "Who the Son sets free is free indeed" (John 8:36). What does freedom mean for you as a believer? Freedom from the need to conform to any worldly value standard, freedom from bondage to addiction, freedom from the need to fulfill what others expect of you, and freedom to pursue His direction for your life.

We touched on the "God-hole" in the last chapter—that empty space in our hearts that can only be filled by identity in Christ and a relationship with Him. At some point in your life, you have probably tried to fill that space with things other than Christ. I know I certainly have tried many things, even though I was raised in the church. But trying to fill a spiritual need with a carnal solution will result in a carnal outcome. This attempt to fill our God-hole with anything other than God is idolatry, pure and simple. Again, I do not say this from a place of condemnation, but from a place of revelation and acceptance. If we understand what idolatry is and the widespread effects it has on the world today, we can properly fight against it and defend our family from it. One of the purest forms of idolatry in today's culture is addiction. Addiction is literally sacrificing a part of yourself to whatever it is that has its hold on you. I touched briefly on my addiction to pornography in a previous chapter. Prior to dealing with that, I also had an addiction to gambling. Furthermore, when working in the casino, I would see people sit at the same blackjack table for hours—even days—compulsively pushing out more money and bigger bets. Addiction is not only real; it is a predatory, powerful, and sneaky master.

As I write about addiction here, I am primarily referring to the addictions that are recognized as issues. I'm not referring to things like addiction to money, achievement, accomplishment, etc. I realize that those can be addictions as well, but I'm not writing with them in mind. That said, much of what we will discuss here can be applied in those less noticeable cases as well.

Addiction begins with self-idolatry and ends with idolizing the act you are addicted to. It may start when you tell yourself that you deserve to indulge a little bit. Or perhaps you dare yourself to try something new, or reassure yourself that it won't hurt to do it just one time. But that is simply where it *starts*. It's easy to move from indulging yourself "just once" to doing it again. Little by little, before you know it, it has become a habit. Then one day, you find yourself no longer doing it for the pleasure, but for the sake of doing it. Even after it has become a compulsive behavior, you may not realize there's a problem. Often you don't see it as a problem until you've made a few attempts to stop.

This is what makes it so sneaky. Concerning identity, addiction is often a sneaky master because it usually tells you to hide your behaviors. At this point, it becomes a hidden identity. I'm talking about the obvious addictions that society has labeled as such. We usually don't hide our addiction to money, fame, power, influence, ambition, or accomplishments, even though those may also set up camp in our lives in an insidious way. It's the addictions that even the world recognizes as bad that we usually hide. And because we hide them, they are very difficult to deal with.

However, make no mistake; addiction is an identity issue at its core. It always reveals an attempt to medicate an area of your life where you lack a sense of security. Furthermore, addiction will always attempt to fill the God-shaped holes you have in your life. When I was stuck in addiction, my thoughts were consumed by it. Even when I wasn't actively engaging in the behavior itself, I was hounded by fantasies of the next time I would have a chance to indulge. The addiction had become who I was. Not who I projected to be to the public, but who I really *was.*

The day came when I realized my addiction had become my master. If you've ever tried to stop a compulsive behavior only to fall right back into it, you understand that you felt like you really didn't have a choice. When you're caught in its grip, it becomes your leader—your taskmaster—and you do what it tells you to do. It may allow you to have other things in your life, like church, family, friends, etc., but it will always bring you back to submission at the altar of addiction.

Addiction vehemently protects itself and its place in your life in various ways.

First, it protects itself through hiding. Why do we hide things from others? Because of shame. Shame results when we engage in something we know we shouldn't. Remember, Adam and Eve's response to their new-found knowledge of sin immediately resulted in shame and hiding. But beware! Keeping an addiction a secret is the most sure-fire way to remain in bondage to it.

Adam and Eve's shame prompted an immediate desire to distance themselves from God. Shame is one of the greatest hindrances to intimacy with Jesus in the Christian faith. You see, as we grow in our knowledge of how sinful we are and our sinful tendencies, we risk letting shame take hold in our lives. If shame has any hold on your life, it will not allow you to fully experience the freedom that Jesus paid for on the cross.

Another way addiction will protect itself is by appearing as a comforter. It deceives you into believing it can offer a solution to your problem. It starts as a fun little indulgence but mutates into a medication for areas of hurt, insecurity, and pain in your life. For example, if you feel disrespected when someone treats you poorly, your addiction tempts you to escape the realities of life.

Addiction is self-preserving. It will find any way to keep even a small amount of itself in your life. Occasionally it will allow you to feel a temporary sense of freedom. Other times it will let you remove it from your life for a season, confident that you will eventually invite it right back into your life, at which point it will be just as strong as it ever was—possibly even stronger.

Addiction highlights why it is so important to have identity in Christ. Once you know who you are in Christ and you understand the huge sacrifice He made for you, you can live a life of freedom through Him. The passionate pursuit of God can set you free from any addiction. Furthermore, allowing your higher identities to rule above your addiction will smother any addictions that have a hold on you. The ultimate goal when you finally break free from addiction is to crush it completely. You see, with Christ as your primary identity, your other identities will automatically fall into place under it: your family roles, your titles, and more.

When I was stuck in my gambling addiction, I came to a point of identity conflict. I had recently been married to the woman of my dreams, which gave me a new-found identity as a husband. I was well aware that being a husband carried a new set of responsibilities. One night after finishing my shift at the casino, I stopped at a neighboring casino to play a few games. I ended up losing $300, which was a lot to me. When I called my new wife and told her about it, I was filled with shame. She did not shame me or condemn me; she only listened and acknowledged it. However, my knowledge of doing wrong filled me with conviction. My realization of the wrong-doing came from my new-found identity as a husband. I reasoned that a husband was not supposed to waste his earnings on a pointless pursuit of money through gambling.

The identity hierarchy took care of the problem like this: I placed my identity of being a good husband above gambling. If I engage in gambling, I'm being irre-sponsible with our money. A good husband is respon-sible with money. Therefore, if I wanted to be a good husband, I could no longer gamble. This is how a sim-ple realization of who you are can destroy an addiction or an idol in your life. After that night, I never gambled in a casino again. If that shame had caused me to hide it rather than being convicted by it, my marriage could have turned out quite different, as you can probably imagine.

So let's bring this back to the matter of your hierar-chy of identities. If identities below your primary iden-tity must fall in line with the primary, addiction has no place in your life once you have established your iden-tity in Christ. So you have to ask yourself the question: Who is the leader? If you're following a compulsive behavior down a particular road, even if you recognize it as detrimental, it is your leader. As Christians, it's foolish to believe we have the ability to lead our own lives. However, even as Christians, we can still fall into addictions quite easily, as in my case. I was raised – and always identified – as a Christian, but I still fell into the trap of addiction. My experience exemplifies the following fact: Christian knowledge is not the same as identity in Christ. You can be a Christian and not live a life led by Christ.

Simply said, everyone is led by something. The question is, *what*? If you find identity in Christ, you will follow Him. But if you're caught up in an addiction, you will follow that addiction.

The notion that we are not free to control our own lives is one that scares the world. However, that knowledge is liberating to those who follow Christ. The fear that identity in Christ might diminish your uniqueness is ludicrous. Quite the opposite is true! It is in Christ that you discover your unique personality and purpose because He has a custom-designed plan for your life! He has called you the salt of the earth. Salt does not diminish the taste of food; it enhances it! Your identity in Christ reveals who you were meant to be.

Identity in Christ allows you to have fun, pursue achievements, attain titles, and enjoy the fruits of this world without finding your value in them.

We can look to King David for an example. God poured out His blessings on David because David had a heart to follow God. When he was caught in sin, David knew that he had sinned against God and God alone. This, of course, does not make sense from a carnal point of view. Had he not sinned against Uriah? Of course! However, the fact that he focused on his sin against God truly points to where David found his identity: it was firmly planted in Christ. When you have identity in Christ, your only focus, and the only leader in your life, is Christ. Every other leader, whether a person or thing, if contradictory to the leading of Christ, must either fall in line with His leading or be eliminated from your life.

As I write these pages, I understand that my words might not come across in the most loving way. I might sound harsh and judgmental. Please know that I'm not suggesting that if you are struggling to rid yourself of an addiction, that means you're not saved. My purpose with this book is not condemnation—it's freedom! Remember, I was stuck in addiction for years. I fully understand the compulsion, helplessness, and shame associated with it. On the other hand, I have also been set free from it. I fully believe it was when I realized my value in Christ and allowed Him to lead my life that I was given the power to leave that life behind.

I would be remiss if I did not invite you to know a life of freedom in Christ. You *can* be set free from any addiction in your life or anything that causes conflict in who you are. You see, when you find identity and value in Christ, you will automatically be faced with the conflict between any addictions that have a hold on you versus your new identity as a child of God. You deserve true freedom—not because I said so, but because God said so when He sent His Son to die on the cross for you. He counted the cost, determined you were worth it, and paid a very high price for you.

Now I want you to evaluate your hierarchy of identity. Determine who the leader is in every situation in your life. Do you find yourself pulled or compelled to engage in a behavior you know is wrong? Do you find yourself getting free from something for a few weeks, maybe even six weeks, and then falling right back into it? If that's happened to you, you know the feeling of shame. Furthermore, you have probably thought that it's not worth trying to quit anymore, because you might fail, and the feeling of failure is miserable.

I know all too well what James 1:14 means when it says our own evil desires drag us away. They drag us back into the things we don't want to do. Have you ever felt like you were being dragged into doing something you knew to be wrong? No doubt about it: that is a cruel and nasty leader.

The worst part of it is when we pervert the written Gospel to deceive ourselves and others into thinking that we're acting in freedom when we partake in sinful acts. That's not freedom! Being ruled by addiction is far from living out the freedom God has designed for you!

You need to understand that when you do things that are contrary to what Christ wants you to do, you are not being led by Christ. It really is as simple as that. To say otherwise, that God is leading you to do sinful acts, is preposterous.

Outbursts of anger, cheating, lying, entertaining lustful thoughts, giving in to jealousy: these are all manifestations of idolatry. They are the polar opposite of what Christ has in store for us when He promised we would have freedom in Him. Furthermore, they indicate that we are allowing something other than Christ to lead us and tell us what to do. To make matters worse, these behaviors are sure to be followed by feelings of shame, condemnation, and oppression.

Remember, *you cannot lead yourself.* Until you come to grips with that statement, you cannot be led by Christ.

Think about a dog named Fido as he follows his owner, Charlie, while they walk down the sidewalk. Now, Charlie does not have a leash, so Fido has the freedom to do as he wishes. When they start, Fido is simply happy to be out for a walk, and he is choosing to follow his owner. Suddenly they encounter another dog across the street who starts barking at Fido. The instant Fido decides to engage with the other dog, he is no longer following Charlie's lead. Charlie is immediately alert to the situation, so before Fido has a chance to bolt across the street, Charlie rebukes him and tells Fido to stay. Fido is then left with a choice: he can either follow his owner or give in to his natural desire to confront the other dog. When Fido decides to ignore his owner's rebuke and run across the street to the other dog, he has decided to allow his fleshly desire to lead him. His instincts are dragging him away from Charlie's good instruction.

You see, Fido did not cease to become Charlie's dog; he simply decided to stop obeying Charlie's direction. This is an example of how we can remain children of God but still not follow His direction for our lives.

This is where the popular anti-legalism argument is problematic.

Many times when someone chooses to follow Christ in today's prominent churches, they are warned against legalism. They are told that their "sin nature" cannot be removed and they don't have to worry about the "little sins" in their lives. After all, they are powerless to remove them. However, they don't realize – and are not taught – that those little sins are actually idols—each and every one of them. And idols can and will be destroyed by following Christ. That's the *only* way idols can be destroyed! The process to eradicate them may take some time, but rest assured, they will be destroyed if you've made the choice to give your entire life to Christ.

If you find yourself doing things you don't want to do, I want to offer you a five-step freedom model.

1. CHOOSE

Choose the leader of your life. Consciously take a moment and make the decision as to who will be in control of your actions. Remember, *it cannot be you*. If your identity is to be found in Christ, you cannot be led by yourself any longer. This is the point where you need to be real with yourself and acknowledge that your choice to engage in habitual sins is a clear indication that you have been led by something other than Christ.

2. PRAY AND BELIEVE

Pray to God in heaven and express your desire to be free. Thank Him for the loving-kindness He has shown you by dying on the cross. Thank Him for the freedom He has bestowed on you by the blood of Jesus. Take a moment of silence to soak in the forgiveness, freedom, and cleansing of your heart. (This step should not be skipped; it's important to bask in the love that He has for you.) Now pour out your thanks to Him for setting you free. And believe that He has set you free indeed.

3. BE ACCOUNTABLE

It's time to tell someone what you were struggling with. If you're a man, you need to find another brother in Christ to talk to about this. Don't wimp out on this part. It's not the same thing if you confess to your wife as your accountability partner. This is about securing true freedom after removing the shame-hold that sin has on your life. This must be done immediately after the freedom Christ just gave you. If you skip this step, your chances of retaining the freedom Christ just gave you are slim. Furthermore, when you speak to your accountability partner, tell him about the freedom you have been given from the addiction. Do not speak of it as a current struggle, because that is no longer your identity. If you're a woman, you should find a woman to be accountable to. The same principle applies; you should not confide in your husband as your accountability partner. This doesn't mean you should not tell your spouse about it, but in seeking freedom, you need to take it to someone else. The light exposes the dirt and allows you to clean it out. Consider this for a moment: have you ever tried to clean a dark room? It's impossible.

4. BUILD THE WALLS

Now it's time to build a wall to protect yourself. Pray earnestly for direction in this area. Take a look at your life and remove everything that tempts you or gives you any cause to fall back. When I eliminated pornography from my life, I had to remove some things from my surroundings and my routines to cleanse my mind. Here are some examples of what God led me to remove immediately upon giving me my freedom.

(Note: these were *my* convictions from the Lord. His direction of what *you* need to remove from your life may look very different.)

Secular television and movies, which are always filled with derogatory messages and sexual situations.

Secular music that often embeds meanings that catch us unawares: we don't even think about the lyrics or all that they insinuate while singing along.

Trips to the gym: I had to stop going to the gym for some time because I was strongly tempted to lust after certain body types.

Now, you might be saying that movies, music, and the gym are not bad things. But that's exactly the point! When you take this step, you're not looking for the *bad* things in your life; you're looking for the things that *cause you to stumble.* On the surface, they may be good things—like going to the gym to be healthy. But whatever they are, you must be alert to anything that drags you down, and then cut them out of your life for the sake of your freedom. At least for a time, those other voices must be silenced.

5. PRESS IN TO GOD

Now is the time to fill yourself with the good things God has given you. Pray and fast. Bask in His presence and the freedom He has given you. My verse for this section is Galatians 5:1: "Stand fast, therefore, in the liberty by which Christ has made us free, and do not be entangled again with a yoke of bondage." We're to stand and revel in the freedom He has given us. Why would we ever choose to be entangled in the yoke of slavery and bondage? It's time to press in to His leading for our lives. Finally, read, pray, fast, and connect. Connect to your local church, find ways to serve, and surround yourself with Christ-centered brothers and sisters.

Finding identity in Christ means freedom from addiction and idolatry. Believe He can set you free and receive it! It may be a process, but He will set you free if you decide to put Him at the top.

I know it may sound harsh to call these "little" sins "idolatry." However, we must address these issues with truth and light. Expose the leaders of your life that persist in contradiction to the Living Word of God. And take heart that it is possible to live in freedom; otherwise, Christ wouldn't continually issue the call to live in freedom throughout the Bible. But we must always remember that this freedom is only found within the dynamic of following our Creator.

12

COMPETITION

HE SAID TO THEM, "YOU ARE THE ONES WHO JUSTIFY YOURSELVES IN
THE EYES OF OTHERS, BUT GOD KNOWS YOUR HEARTS. WHAT PEOPLE
VALUE HIGHLY IS DETESTABLE IN GOD'S SIGHT."
LUKE 16:15

Throughout my time in the Marines, I did well by Marine Corps standards. This means I had high physical fitness scores, did excellent work in my field, and took continuing education courses, which were optional. Each of these pursuits are things the Marine Corps leadership looks at when considering someone for a promotion. To transition from Lance Corporal to Corporal and Corporal to Sergeant, you must be at the top of your field in these areas, among other factors. In my military occupational specialty, rising through the ranks was a slow process in my first few years, because they didn't need any more Corporals in my job. Therefore, even though my score was quite high in all of the qualifying areas, I had to wait three years to become a Corporal. During the time that my field was closed for promotion, all I could do was continue to do well and build up my status and rank among my peers. That way when an opportunity for promotion opened up, I would be in prime position to be considered.

Imagine my disappointment when I ranked 6th among hundreds of Lance Corporals in my field when the day finally came, and they only promoted the top five to Corporal. To add more context without going into too much detail about the process, my score was over 1700 points, and I missed the mark by less than 10 points. It was heartbreaking, to say the least.

What was the Marine Corps telling me? It was telling me that according to my works, I was not quite valuable enough to become a Corporal—not yet. My promotion would have to wait a little longer. Others had won out over me for various reasons.

You see, my value to the Marine Corps was determined by what I did to better myself as a Marine. But this was also a life of competition. Those who were physically gifted and knew the point accrual game the best had an edge. Because my value in the Marines was determined by the points I could accrue, every other Marine in my rank was a competitor.

In competition, there are winners and losers. In a large pool of people, the competition can be fierce when only one or very few will attain the prize. When we allow our identity to be defined by career success, titles, education, or achievements, our life will be one long and monotonous competition. Our pursuit of those ahead of us will be never-ending, and our feeling of superiority towards those behind us will tarnish our spirits.

It's important to understand the principle of competition and the role it plays in our lives. If our value is determined by the results of competition, we will always be vying for position and power. Consider a scenario where my value is determined by my title. Then, when I enter a room full of people, I must find out everyone else's title to determine my standing among them. With this as my mindset, I'm putting myself in constant competition with those around me.

Now, before you start to think I'm disparaging competition, let me clarify. In general, competition is a good thing. It can bring out the best in us. Competition is often fun, exhilarating, and meaningful. Some of us use competition as a means to motivate ourselves to become better versions of ourselves. It is certainly an integral piece of our society. It allows us to assess the value of a company, an organization, or a team. Without competition, most people, businesses, and teams would not strive for excellence in life. Therefore, at its core, competition is a good thing.

The danger comes when you define your individual value by competitive standards, comparing yourself to others.

The negative effects of competition come up when we start to view the winner as more valuable than the loser. That mentality says the more successful you become, the more valuable you are as a person. If you find your primary identity in your success, you will stay in competition. You may have been taught to look at your bank accounts and determine that your net worth in the bank indicates your worth as a person. However, that is a worldly view of your worth, not God's view.

When living a life of competition, at some point you will make one of two choices.

1) You will either settle for a level of achievement that you can be content with, all the while knowing others are ahead of you.

2) You will continue chasing that next level of achievement, whether title, success, money, or any

other form of validation that gives your soul a sense of value.

Let me illustrate to explain.

When we progress through the levels of higher education, we attain various degrees: associate's, bachelor's, master's, and doctorate. Most people who attend college do not go beyond a bachelor's degree for many valid reasons. If someone finds their value or identity in their level of education, they must come to a point where they are okay with not being at the top of the educational ladder. Those who place their value in their education level but do not have the time or energy to go on to attain their master's or doctorate, must either come to terms with the idea that they are not as valuable as they could be, or they must find a way to continue to pursue the graduate programs. So if one determines his value in terms of his level of education, and they have not decided on a point where they will be satisfied with attaining that level, they cannot stop at a bachelor's or master's without admitting they are not valuable enough. (This is a mindset I'm talking about, not the truth.) Furthermore, even when they earn a doctorate, there are always further certifications, etc. that can further define your educational value. This is the problem with finding your value in these things. You will always find someone who has a higher value than you do.

Let's go back to my story of when I was trying to attain the rank of Corporal while in the Marine Corps. After achieving that rank, I had an opportunity to take what's called "Corporal's Course." This is a training course designed to help Corporals become better leaders. I applied but I was not selected because I had declared my intention not to stay in the Military after my first enlistment. For that reason, they chose to send other Corporals who had not expressed their intention to exit the Military.

I was angry about their decision not to allow me to receive further training. When I vented my frustration to a buddy of mine, he asked me a simple question. "Why would you want to go anyway?" We both knew how strenuous the course was, and how it wasn't meant to be a fun time. The question caught me off-guard. So I gave him a gut reaction.

"Because I don't want any other Corporals to have a leg up on me."

You see, I was operating from a spirit of competition. The hard work I had put in to attain my rank was a badge of honor for me. However, that rank was not enough when there were other things I could achieve to distinguish myself among my peers. It bothered me that others of my rank could receive training beyond the training that was available to me. It wouldn't change anything substantial like my pay, but it was a mark of something exclusive. It would distinguish the other Corporals above me—if only in my mind. When my value was found in my success, everyone else was a competitor and there would always be someone more valuable than me in that context.

In economics, value is determined by the consumer's willingness to pay. When my wife and I were shopping for a new television recently, we had a decision to make. On one hand, we found a TV at the size we wanted for $350, but it was made by a brand we did not recognize. Then there was the Vizio of the same size for $500. The TV we already had was a Vizio, and we trusted their brand, but the lower price was tempting.

However, we valued the Vizio brand enough to pay the extra amount, and went home happy.

What was it that made the Vizio $150 more valuable than the other? To break it down to the basic principle, we valued their brand enough and were willing to pay the additional amount. The value was determined by our willingness to pay. Now say we had gone with the $350 television. Also, imagine no one else was willing to pay the extra $150 for the Vizio brand. That would mean the Vizio was not worth $500. Now, the specifications of the television would not have changed, nor the functionality. Nothing material would have changed about the television; the only thing that would have changed in this scenario would have been the consumer's willingness to pay for it. Generally speaking, the consumer's willingness to pay is what determines the value of a good or service.

In life, we try to make ourselves more valuable by attaining experience, education, money, and material things. This is not necessarily a bad thing. In fact, it's necessary if you're playing the business or corporate ladder game. However, the danger comes when these things determine your own perception of your personal value—and when you start to determine the value of others based on these factors.

There must become a distinction in your mind between your value in the marketplace and your value as a person.

Comparison culture tells us the amount of money we make, the education we achieve, the titles we possess, or the cars we drive make us more or less valuable than the next person in all contexts. The value that a job attaches to us is valid for assessing our worth in the context of the workforce because a company or clientele will pay us according to their assessment of our value. You see, we do have a value in the context of worldly structures, but the danger comes when the values created by those structures determine the way we see ourselves and others on a personal level.

Let's come back to the question of your worth using the economic principle. The fundamental Christian belief is that Jesus died on the cross for the sins of the world. Think about it in terms of how value is determined. You are worth what someone is willing to pay for you, right? Therefore, in your case, that value was determined some 2,000 years ago when Jesus paid the ultimate price for you on the cross.

1 Corinthians 6:20 says, "You were bought at a price." The price that purchased you was the absolute highest price that could ever be paid. This is why it's so important to assess your value and the value of others by the price Jesus paid for you. You can gain the highest titles in your industry and have billions of dollars in your bank account, but nothing will ever compare to the price that the Lord placed on your life all those years ago.

Your value and mine are the exact same as that of the homeless man on the street corner and the CEO of the biggest company you can think of. Our value was determined on the cross. It is fixed and cannot fluctuate. Your past mistakes, your current situation, your ministry, or the way people treat you has no bearing on your value because it can never change. Your value cannot go up or down. You can diminish your view of your value, but that doesn't change your actual value, because Christ died for all.

AND HE DIED FOR ALL, THAT THOSE WHO LIVE SHOULD NO LONGER LIVE FOR THEMSELVES BUT FOR HIM WHO DIED FOR THEM AND WAS RAISED AGAIN. 2 CORINTHIANS 5:15.

Let me invite you to do something for yourself now: say these words out loud: *"Jesus died for me. I am a child of God, bought at the highest price possible."*

Did you say it out loud? Do you believe it?

Let's try it again. *Read it aloud!* If you're in public, just whisper: *"Jesus died for me. I am a child of God, bought at the highest price possible."*

You were bought at the highest price possible by the blood of your sinless God in human form. Your value is set forever. Jesus indeed died for everyone, but here's *your* truth: He died specifically for *you*, not just for everyone. Contemplate the implications of this and make the distinction in your mind between Him dying for *everyone* and Him dying for *you*. He died specifically for you because He decided that you—yes, you—specifically you—were worth the cost.

You can make yourself more valuable at your job, you can make yourself more valuable to your spouse, and you can make yourself more valuable for your country, but you can never make yourself a more valuable child of God. Your value has already been set at the highest price possible.

13

JUST AS A BODY, THOUGH ONE, HAS MANY PARTS, BUT ALL ITS
MANY PARTS FOR ONE BODY, SO IT IS WITH CHRIST.
1 CORINTHIANS 12:12

A ministry identity is usually defined by the title or the position one holds in the church. It may be assigned by the leadership or earned through experience or service. I want to explore some roles, positions, and actions that give us identity in the body of Christ within a church structure. Is your identity in the church the same as your identity in Christ? I would contest they are meant to be quite different things, but that is something only you can decide in your walk with God – and your answer may depend on the season of life you are in. However, even if they are different identities, they still must fall in line with one another and work hand-in-hand. So let's dive in.

Prior to actively serving in our local church, I often struggled with the concept of "service." I heard it routinely from others in the church, and it usually felt a little condescending when someone would ask my wife and me to serve in some area of ministry. The request always seemed to imply that we needed to pull our weight. We were not "serving" in the church because, at the time, we owned and operated a business during the week. By the time the weekend came around, we were exhausted and completely drained. Furthermore, we saw many people come to Christ and grow closer to Him through our business, so we felt confident that our field of service was in business. That's where we felt God had called us to promote and advance the Kingdom of God. We had also brought quite a few of our clients to the church, and they became active members. For this reason, we didn't feel the need to serve within the church itself. Our ministry identity was not found in serving in the church building. I'm not saying this line of thinking was right or wrong; I'm simply expressing our motives at the time.

Fast forward to now. These days, I love serving in the church. Whether it's leading a life group, helping to stack chairs, working with the children, or handing out flyers—wherever I'm needed, it's a joy to be an active part of the organization. However, these actions do not give me an identity in Christ; they are a manifestation of my identity in Christ. I serve because I love Christ, I don't love Christ because I serve.

It is important to distinguish our identity in Christ from our identity in the church institution. Any identity other than our identity in Christ has the potential to become a source of great pride. And once we learn to distinguish the two, we must make sure they are in line with one another.

Some churches place a heavy emphasis on serving in the church. To a great extent, the church relies on volunteer support from its members. I'm not condemning this; it's simply an observation. Tithing and giving to the church can only offer so much practical support. The church also needs people who are willing to sacrifice some of their time to help the church reach more people and grow. However, in my opinion, the church as an institution has almost attempted to take ownership of the word "serve," supporting the erroneous notion that if you're not serving in your church, you're not serving.

Serving is not limited to the church as an institution in any way. This is not the restriction placed on the word "serve."

Although most of us know intuitively that serving is not limited to the church, serving is still often used within the exclusive context of serving within the confines of the church institution. You must reject that limiting belief. I believe to fully move into your identity in Christ, you must not allow the church institution to define the meaning of service in your mind.

Another reason churches emphasize service is to encourage their members to be active and generate a feeling of pride in the church. In an earlier chapter, I explored the concept of organizations using titles as a means to give subordinates a sense of importance. Remember Dwight from The Office? Titles convey expectations. Therefore, there are expectations associated with titles in ministry: the roles we are to play and specific forms of service attached to each role. Service within these roles can give us a sense of our importance within an organization.

For example, when my wife and I started helping with the children's ministry, we were expected to be there for each service during the time we had committed to serving. The expectation was clear – be there on time ready to work – and we were expected to live up to it.

Ministry identities give us a reason to commit to the church.

Some of us need that extra boost of motivation to get up and drive to the church every weekend. Otherwise, we might just take a week off from church here or there just because we don't feel up for the 10-minute drive.

Is there a danger in finding identity in man-made positions and titles, even in the church? Perhaps. Of course, that depends on the position in the hierarchy where that identity falls for you personally.

A high identity in the institutional church can be very risky for your faith if placed above your identity in Christ. If you've ever witnessed a prominent church leader fall into some form of immorality, you know it can be devastating to the congregation. Many people within the church turn away from their faith altogether after such an occurrence. I believe that in some cases, people within the congregation fall away because they placed too high a value on their identity relative to the church staff and the institution of the church itself. This is why I say it is dangerous to attach too much importance to your identity in the church organization. When the organizational structure fails, your faith can waver.

It's natural and good to find identity within any organization, and I'm certainly a proponent of serving in your local church. The problem comes when we place too much emphasis there and find our value in our position in the church, our title, or the service we perform there. If our title is a source of pride, or if we consider ourselves more valuable than others who are not "serving," we need to reevaluate our identity hierarchy.

Think about the following: if you take time out of your weekend to serve in the church, you have made yourself more valuable to that institution. In other words, your actions and works have elevated your worth within the institution. Your works directly affect your value in the church. On the other hand, your works can never affect your value in Christ. Therefore, I must conclude they are quite different identities.

Everyone has a different role to play within the body of Christ, and everyone is in a different season of life. For example, the mother of two toddlers might not have the energy or the time to put herself out there and work at the church on her weekends. And if she does, her focus might be too divided to dive in the way the leadership would want her to.

This is why church leadership must be careful not to pressure individuals into serving out of guilt or a sense of obligation. We all have a series of commitments apart from our duty to the church: obligations we must fulfill to our family, our job, or our community. We also have different energy levels.

Paul summarizes this principle very clearly in Romans 12:3-8:

"For by the grace given me I say to every one of you: Do not think yourself more highly than you ought, but rather think of yourself with sober judgment, in accordance with the faith God has granted to each of you. For just as each of us has *one body* with many members, and *these members do not all have the same function*, so in Christ, we, though many, form one body, and each member belongs to all the others. We have different gifts, according to the grace given to each of us. If your gift is prophesying, then prophesy in accordance with your faith; if it is serving, then serve; if it is teaching,

then teach; if it is to encourage, then give encourage-
ment; if it is giving, then give generously; if it is to lead,
do it diligently; if it is to show mercy, do it cheerfully."
(Emphasis added.)

In these verses, we see Paul express how God values the person who simply encourages right along
with the person who gives. These are not all gifts that
are necessarily viewed as valuable to a church from an
external viewpoint, but they are certainly valuable to
a healthy body of Christ. For some, simply showing up
may be all they can muster in their season of life, and
that does not make them less valuable as a member
of the body of Christ. Our value must be continually
found in Christ, not in the church as an institution or
even our relationship with the pastor.

Paul drives his point home even further in 1 Corinthians 12 when talking about the gifts of the Spirit.
Once again, using the analogy of the body, Paul de-
scribes how silly it is for your foot to be considered
less valuable than the hand because it doesn't serve the
same function. We must carefully refrain from using
our service in the church to project onto others what
they should be doing for the church.

The reason for the church, as the body of Christ, is
the edification and support for one another. The institution of support and identity is important for many
social and spiritual reasons. The need for the church
and the reason the church exists is extremely valuable.
The church is there to serve the people just as Christ
came to serve.

We are all one body, made up of different parts.
And each part is important to the whole. However,
when we start looking at other people's positions within the ministry and compare our service to theirs, we

have lost sight of the reason for the church, and we've focused on service to the church. Many in the church serve out of legalism, thinking their service gives them a leg up on those who don't serve. This negates the value of service.

To choose to serve means to place yourself in a position lower than the rest of the crowd. To be clear, that does not diminish your value; it's a position. In serving those in your local church, you have the opportunity to step into the same role Jesus did when He washed His disciples' feet.

By definition, when we serve, we place ourselves in a position beneath those whom we serve. So when someone takes pride in their service, it diminishes any benefit they would receive from serving. Jesus didn't serve His disciples for recognition or a feeling of belonging; He did it to demonstrate how we are to serve one another with a servant's heart.

In Matthew 6, Jesus gives us guidelines for service to others. In verse 2 He says, "So when you give to the needy, do not announce it with trumpets, as the hypocrites do in the synagogues and on the streets to be honored by others. Truly I tell you, they (the hypocrites) have received their reward in full." He goes on to present other examples of those who call attention to their service to impress others. He is very clear on this point: If you are seeking to be recognized or honored by others in your service, you have already received your reward.

This means that their recognition *is* your reward.

That doesn't seem so bad, I suppose, if you don't trust that God *does* reward that which is done in secret. But when we know the awesome power of God to rule and direct our lives, we know that any reward from Him is far greater than the mere recognition of man.

Finally, let me alert you to the danger of using ministry in the church as an excuse to not serve beyond the church. As Christians, we can fall into the "I did my time in church, so I'm good for this week" trap. You must understand that serving in the church does not excuse you from serving elsewhere throughout the week. Your service must not be confined within the four walls of the church. Jesus called you to a life of service and helping others (Ephesians 2:10).

How can I think that I have paid my dues with a little bit of service on the weekend when I owe Jesus so much? Don't be confused by this statement; serving God by serving people is not a legalistic thing. This is living out of the calling Christ has set on your life and mine. And living in His calling is far greater and more joyful than any plans I could ever make for my own life. Ministry is an all-day-every-day thing. This is why it's so important for us as Christians to carry ourselves in a manner that reflects the image of Christ.

When our identity is in Christ, we cannot look down on our fellow man. It is impossible to have a godly view of the world and devalue other humans for whom Jesus died. You cannot serve as Jesus served if you think your service makes you better than the people you are serving.

Again, it is a good thing to be involved in your local church. However, I implore you to make sure you are doing it with the right heart. Serving in your church is an opportunity to work alongside Christ in humility and joy. It should bring joy and a feeling of closeness with your Heavenly Father. If at any time pride creeps in or you start to feel as if you're doing God a favor with your service, it may be time to reevaluate your identity priority. Don't allow your service in the church to override your identity as a child of God.

Furthermore, your church leadership will benefit—and be grateful—if you serve with a true servant's heart. The willingness to do what's needed for the collective good of your church family is an asset and a valuable role to play in the overall mission of the church organization.

Our identity within ministry is important, but it is far more important to find identity in Christ. The reason I'm convinced that these identities are separate is because there are many different roles within a church, but only one Christ. We all have the same identity in Christ, but not all the same identity—or role to play—within the organization or body of Christ. God gave each of us gifts that are unique to us. It is important to submit our gifts to Him so that He might use them to benefit the church. But make no mistake: our identity is not defined by the benefit to the church; it is defined by His blood on the cross.

14

THE SPIRIT OF THE SOVEREIGN LORD IS ON ME, BECAUSE THE LORD HAS ANOINTED ME TO PROCLAIM GOOD NEWS TO THE POOR. HE HAS SENT ME TO BIND UP THE BROKENHEARTED, TO PROCLAIM FREEDOM FOR THE CAPTIVES AND RELEASE FROM DARKNESS FOR THE PRISONERS.
ISAIAH 61:1

A few days ago, I went to the gym early in the morning, as I usually do before work. This particular morning, as I removed my jacket to begin my workout, I noticed a large messy smear on my white T-shirt—a spaghetti stain? *Oh, no!* Immediately, a little voice inside my head screamed, *How embarrassing! Quick, put your jacket back on. Go to the bathroom and see if you can wash it out. You can't let these people see that!*

However, this feeling of embarrassment lasted only a split second; I continued with my workout as normal, stain and all.

Why was I able to be free of that embarrassment so quickly? After all, a few short years ago, my reaction would have been very different.

The reason I could let go of the embarrassment is because I'm a parent of two toddlers. You see, when you become a parent, there are certain things you can get away with because you now carry that title. This new identity sets you free of the need to be clean all the time. The parents of toddlers get a pass when it comes to being late to social events. They are not judged for drinking too much coffee. They are not expected to have a clean house when company comes over. (In fact, it's usually a little weird if a house with small children is clean.) Becoming a parent sets you free from many social obligations and judgments.

When you become a parent, you are set free from several expectations that used to be in place, or that you *thought* were in place for you before you had children. Becoming a parent of small children gave me a new identity—one that set me free!

When I noticed the stain on my shirt, I knew it had come from one of my little girls. Therefore, I felt no shame, and I didn't wonder if onlookers would think I was a dirty person. (As if anyone's looking anyway, but let's play along.) If they are a parent, they probably know where the stain came from. And if they aren't a parent, it really doesn't matter, because *I* know where it came from. This new identity protects me from feeling embarrassed. As long as I am content knowing that I'm a parent and that the spaghetti stain is almost like a badge, I won't be shamed by others for something that comes along with the territory of parenting.

At that moment, I had an epiphany. I realized that some identities bring us under the bondage of condemnation and others set us free. This is immediately applicable to my identity in Christ. When I know who I am in Christ my Savior and see myself as a child of God, that identity—believing in Him—automatically sets me free from the bondage of sin. It sets me free from trying to prove that I'm a good Christian. It sets me free from having to prove that I'm better than unbelievers.

As you get deeper into this idea, true identity in Christ sets us free from being judged and from judging others. How can we judge a brother or sister when we realize how much Christ forgave us when He died on the cross?

When we feel this kind of freedom, we know that we have been set free from one or more identities that had enslaved us.

What does it mean to be enslaved by an identity? Well, simply put, when an identity that seems admirable is misinterpreted, it can easily enslave us if we place too high a priority on it.

For example, a man who provides well for his family might value his worth as a good provider so highly that it becomes his identity as a husband and father. However, if maintaining that role involves working extremely long hours, he risks falling into the trap of neglecting his wife and children and ensuring that they receive the love and attention they desperately need from him. As a result, he will spend longer hours at work because he finds his highest identity in his role as a provider.

Although providing financially for his family is a good thing, it must be managed correctly. If it becomes the number one focus of his life, other things will suffer. He won't allow himself to take a little extra time off work for special occasions, games, parties, or date nights—because that would mean taking time away from work.

This man has stripped down his role in life, or his identity, to being a "good family man." But is his definition justified? Here is the equation he has come up with:

A good man = a good provider.

A good provider = more money.

More money = more time at work.

He reasons that time spent at work validates his identity as a "good man." Can you see how this identity has come to enslave him? His commitment to that role and its implications means he is not free to do as he pleases with his time. If he must choose between going to his child's dance recital or spending more time at work, which one do you think he will choose? You got it! He will likely forego the recital and put in a few extra hours at work. Sure, he would *like* to support his child by attending her recital, but the mantra in his head repeats: "A good man provides for his family; therefore he does not always get to do what he wants to do."

Other enslaving identities can be found in our attention to outward appearance. Of course, we all agree that it's important to be presentable, hygienic, and to live clean and healthy lifestyles. However, it's possible to so anchor our identity in these things that this mindset becomes counterproductive in our life.

For example, imagine a mother of three small children preparing to have guests over to the house. She considers herself a good mother, and always makes sure that her appearance reflects that identity. As the time draws near for the company to arrive, she realizes the house is a complete disaster. She cannot allow the guests to see it like this because they might think she is a terrible mother who cannot manage her children. So she sets out to clean up the house as quickly as possible. Now, you may be thinking this is a good thing. But imagine in the midst of cleaning up she begins to scream at her children, belittle them, and call them names. Her frustration cannot be contained because the messy house has challenged her identity as a good mother. When her projected identity is challenged, the equation towards protecting it looks something like this:

A good mother = children in order.

Children in order = a clean and clear house.

A messy house = challenge to her identity as a good mother.

This woman finds her highest identity in life as being perceived as a good mother. In her mind, this means everyone must see her "put together," in control of her surroundings, and having children who obey her. By contrast, a dirty house would reveal to the guests that she is not a good mother – by her own standard. When the love of her children and caring for their feelings come secondary to the appearance she feels obligated to protect, her focus on conforming to the *image* of "a good mother" has become a hindrance to actually *being* a good mother.

When we think about it in these terms, it's easy to dismiss, but this happens in many areas of our lives. Someone wants to show the world how successful they are, so they buy an expensive car that enslaves them in a life of debt. A young couple wants to announce to the world their love and commitment to one another by starting their journey off with an expensive wedding and honeymoon. But that choice builds their marriage on a foundation of debt and financial irresponsibility.

The list goes on and on.

What we don't often realize in these cases is this: this type of projection is *not a true identity* – it represents an attempt to control the way others see us.

Rather than actually choosing to be a nice person for the sake of being nice, we find identity in *behaving* like a nice person so that others will *perceive* us as being nice. What a stressful pursuit! When you get caught in this never-ending cycle, what others think about you becomes your top priority. Trying to maintain your identity through the expectations and perceptions of others is more than stressful – It's exhausting!

When we boil it down, the identities that enslave us often reveal our efforts to please others and to impress them by protecting an artificial self-image. When we get so wrapped up in defining our value in terms of the way others perceive us, it can be a very stressful, dangerous, and tumultuous way to live. Sadly, that is how many people live from day-to-day.

Back to my dirty shirt. You see now how my previous concern that others see me as a clean person was overridden by the true and more important identity of being a parent. It doesn't matter if the people who see me in my dirty shirt know that I'm a parent because *I* know I'm a parent—and that supersedes anything that others think or know. If my identity were determined by the way others viewed me, then I might still be embarrassed by a stained shirt. However, considering my identity as a parent to be more important than my image in others' eyes has set me free from that embarrassment and condemnation.

There are times when an identity that is generally considered commendable can turn out to be one that enslaves us. When we confuse identity in Christ with identity in good works, we throw ourselves back into bondage.

This is the difference between identity in Christ and legalism. Entrusting your identity to Christ sets you free from your past, free from condemnation, and free from the slavery of sin. Legalism puts you in bondage to the rules you are "supposed" to follow, shackles you in condemnation, and asks you to constantly compete with sin by outweighing the bad things in your life with good.

If you become a slave to a legalistic mindset, you will constantly worry about what others think of you. You will agonize over "doing the right thing" to uphold the image you want to project – and protect – rather than doing it for the sake of acting honorably. On the other hand, when you focus on your identity in Christ, your desire to do the right thing is not attached to ulterior motives or your concern for approval from others. Identity in Christ allows us to do the right thing without being obligated to it.

This shows that a true identity in Christ has the power to set you free from the bondage of legalism and rules. True identity in Christ motivates you to follow the rules but releases you from the need to be bound by them.

Let's take a moment to consider religious rituals. In and of themselves, they are usually not bad. But it's possible to be legalistic about anything. Rituals can become problematic when they are placed in the incorrect priority. For example, if you find yourself showing up at church every time the doors are open just so that others will see how pious you are, that is a ritual bordering on legalism.

We can be legalistic about anything. And I really do mean *anything.* If it is done for the purpose of being viewed a certain way or an attempt to gain more favor in God's sight, it's legalism.

Wow! Think about it. You can be legalistic about being nice. Legalism is not the act itself or even the ritual, it's the context of your mindset.

If your identity in Christ carries more importance than your preoccupation with your religious rituals, you will do the right things for the right reasons.

Does this mean we never do bad things? No.

What it means is when you do something bad, you're not acting in your true identity found in Christ.

When you know who you are in Christ, you will not be bound by other's opinions and perceptions. It doesn't matter what other people in the church think of you, what your neighbors think of you, or what your family thinks of you. The only thing that matters is Jesus gave His life for you, you belong to Him, and you're a son or daughter of the Most High God.

When you feel motivated to please Him with your works, you will do them regardless of who is watching.

It's important to note that Scripture is quite clear on this point: a true identity in Him will produce good works every time (James 2:14-20). However, the reverse is not true. Good works cannot give you identity in Christ or save your soul.

I'll say that again. *Identity in Christ always produces good works, but good works cannot produce identity in Christ.*

Identity in Christ is not the only identity that gives us freedom from some things, but it is the only one that gives us freedom from *everything*: any situation, circumstance, past sins, addiction, anger, or any other bondage that has you in its grip. A true identity in Christ can *and will* set you free from all of that.

Knowing that you are a child of God—a beloved adopted child of The King—sets you free! No person or thing on this earth can take that away from you. When someone confronts you with the obligation to be doing something, or going somewhere, or abstaining from one thing or another, you can look them in the eye and say, "Thank you for that suggestion," and move on with your life.

Their opinion of you is not your reality. Their opinion of you is not your identity.

Nobody gets to choose your identity for you except you. Who will have the privilege of determining your identity? Will you give that prerogative to other people? Or give it to Christ? Trust me, only one of those choices can end well for you.

15

ALIGNED WITH CHRIST

DO NOT CONFORM TO THE PATTERN OF THIS WORLD, BUT BE TRANSFORMED
BY THE RENEWING OF YOUR MIND. THEN YOU WILL BE ABLE TO TEST AND
APPROVE WHAT GOD'S WILL IS – HIS GOOD, PLEASING AND PERFECT WILL.
ROMANS 12:2

Throughout the previous chapters, we've explored how the various identities in our lives control and dictate our decisions and actions. In light of this principle, it is critically important to fully understand the identities at work in us and to anchor our primary identity in Christ. Aligning our thinking to the principles Christ has given us to live by removes the primary sources of conflict in our minds. Giving our lives to Him involves submitting our decision-making to the leading of the Holy Spirit. Allowing God to be the decision-maker guarantees a better outcome 100% of the time. When we have identity in Christ, our thoughts become more clear, our decisions become much easier, and we can live in peace within ourselves knowing He is in control.

Nevertheless, it's important to know that you will always struggle with conflicting identities, even when you have identity in Christ. You see, conflicting identities arise when tough decisions must be made. When you are under a lot of pressure, various thoughts will go through your mind as to how you should react to the pressure. What is the best response when faced with a challenging situation? Should you be aggressive and proactive? Should you put up your defenses? Silently stand your ground? Retreat and find another way? How do you know when you are making the right decision?

Because we play many roles in life, each representing one of our many identities, it is not uncommon to find our identities jousting with each other in the face of a particularly challenging decision. In the extreme, it can feel as if a war is being waged in our minds. In this context, conflicting identities often plague us with doubts, which further complicates the process of arriving at a life decision that is well-reasoned, sound, and based on God's wisdom.

Conflicting identities – although natural and inescapable – always have a tendency to cause doubts and insecurities to well up inside us. This is why knowledge of the conflicting identities principle is so important.

When God instructed my wife and me to pick up our family and move from California to Colorado, it was very abrupt. God's direction to move was clear (move immediately), but the details were not. The questions that came to mind were endless. The provider in me said, "How are you going to support your family?" After all, God was asking us to make the move with no job lined up, no house, and no family or friends in Colorado. Another voice pelted me, demanding, "What about your friends here? You don't know anyone in Colorado who can help you with your little girls." (Our girls were two years old and six months old at the time.)

I'm not going to pretend that my stress level didn't rise during the move. However, we had heard from God that this was the correct decision. The knowledge that it was His decision made it easier because it was certainly not a decision we would have made on our own. As a protector of my family, I felt a deep need to ensure that my family felt safe and secure. Each of my identities was popping up with questions. But the conflicts and doubts that arose from all those identities were subdued by my desire to follow Christ. I was confident that His decisions for my life – and my family – would be much better than any plans I could come up with.

I know having identity conflicts sounds like a terrible thing. However, as I read through the Bible, it is clear to me that this is normal, even in our walk with the Lord. Let's look at some of the anecdotes about the disciples. It's apparent that when they deferred to the wrong identities amid a pressing decision, these little conflicts led to them doing some pretty dumb stuff.

We all love the stories about Peter in the Bible. Some of us love him because we can relate to him. Peter was a tough guy. He said what was on his mind, and he was not afraid of offending anyone. When it was time to fight, he was the guy you wanted in your corner. We also find evidence that he was a survivor. Furthermore, Peter was undoubtedly a fervent follower of Christ. However, he often allowed his other identities to control his decision-making.

Here are some examples:

In Matthew chapter 16, we read about Peter acting in two different identities, seemingly within the same day. When Jesus asked His disciples who they said He was, Peter was the one who spoke up, saying, "You are the Christ, the Son of the living God" (verse 16). Then just a little while later, Jesus explained that He was going to have to die in Jerusalem. Guess who was there to rebuke the Christ, the Son of the living God? Yup, the same man: Peter. Moments after being fully connected to God and having a divine revelation about who Jesus was, he pulled Jesus aside and had the audacity to rebuke Him. Why would he do such a thing? At that moment, he had laid aside his identity as a follower of Christ and was acting instead as a protector. Peter saw himself as the tough guy who was there to protect Jesus and fight for Him. Peter's identity as the protector compelled him to take control and assure Jesus that he would never allow that to happen to Him. As a protector, he openly questioned Jesus' decision. Furthermore, he was not only *questioning* His decision; he was attempting to *take over* the decision making. He proceeded to tell Jesus that this would never happen to Him.

Jesus responded to Peter with one of the most confusing commands. "Get behind me, Satan!" What? Was Jesus calling Peter Satan? I've heard a few explanations of this dialogue, but one thing is clear: Peter was not acting according to his identity in Christ. Jesus went on to tell Peter, "You do not have in mind the concerns of God, but merely human concerns." Now that was a pretty big statement, given that Peter had been following Jesus for the last three years. First, Peter received divine revelation from God, then moments later Jesus rebuked him, saying he was only concerned with human problems. We know Peter wasn't stuck in that "human concerns" mindset all the time. However, in the heat of that high-pressure situation, Peter's identity as the protector rose to the surface and drove his reaction to Jesus' disturbing news.

We can find other examples of Peter acting outside his identity in Christ. Just a short while after rebuking Jesus, he decided once again that as His protector, he would cut off the ear of one of the men who had come to arrest Jesus (tough guy – protector). Later that same night, after claiming he would die for Jesus, he denied that he even knew Him when recognized and confronted as a follower of Jesus (survivor).

Those identity issue conflicts don't stop for Peter – even after Jesus' death. Later, in Galatians 2:11-14, Paul says he rebuked Peter for trying to conform to the expectations imposed by the Jews in Antioch. In this case, we see Peter controlled by the perceived expectation from other Jews as to who he was supposed to eat with as a Jew. In other words, as a Jew, Peter knew who he was – and was not – expected to sit and dine with. By Paul's account, Peter's decision of who he would sit with changed the moment the other Jews arrived. Therefore, his actions were controlled by his attempt to protect his Jewish identity.

We all know Peter as one of the greatest disciples and apostles. I'm not just trying to take stabs at him. However, these stories should provide some clarity and hope for the situations you and I face every day. You see, there are times when it's natural to allow other identities to take precedence in the midst of making a decision. However, it is possible to 'take every thought captive' (2 Corinthians 10:5) and thus bring all of these identities into submission to our identity in Christ. This is why Paul tells us not to conform to the ways of the world but to be transformed by the renewing of our minds (Romans 12:2).

By the way, Peter is not the only disciple who acts outside of his identity in Christ. (And no, I'm not talking about Judas.) Let's look at a couple of other examples.

In Matthew 20:20-24, the mother of James and John came to Jesus, asking that He might seat her two sons on His right and His left when He took His throne. James and John were not following Christ in that instance. They were following worldly desires for power and title. They wanted the position of second in command next to Jesus. They were following the identity their mother wanted to project onto them rather than following Christ's purpose.

Now let's look at what happened when Jesus died. All the disciples gathered together in fear. They apparently did not believe Him when He told them He would rise from the dead. Thomas took it a step further, adding that he would never believe unless he touched the scars from the cross. It had to be scary, knowing that Jesus had left them. At that time, when apprehension and the unknown were mixed with doubt, the disciples reacted in worldly survival mode. Losing the man, Jesus, meant losing their identity as followers of Christ. How hard it must have been to face so much uncertainty!

This last example is a great testament to why it is so essential for you to find your identity in Christ and not in people in the ministry. Yes, you will usually identify with a church or a ministry leader here on Earth, but that identity should in no way impact your faith in Christ.

When opposing identities come into conflict, one identity must win out. Therefore, you must daily commit to your identity in Christ as your lead identity. If you can allow your identity as a follower of Christ to direct you and guide you through the day, your decisions will become much easier. It's a little worn out by now, but you can always go back to the saying, "What would Jesus do?" If the answer to that question serves as your watchword and guides your thinking as you go through your day, that is one indicator that you are anchoring your top identity in Christ.

If you desire to remove conflict from your life and make your decisions easier, you need a supreme decision-maker in your life. Think about how a group of children acts when left to their own devices. Without an adult to guide them, they will often begin to squabble and fight. Furthermore, they may get into trouble, dabbling in unsafe activities. Children need a leader to watch over them, guide them, and keep them safe.

As children of God, we are no different from that group of unruly children. We need His direction and guidance. However, just as with a group of children, each of whom has a mind of his own, it is not always easy to submit to His will for our lives. Until you come to terms with the fact that His decisions for your life are far better than anything you can comprehend, you will not enjoy the fullness of what He has in store for you. On the other hand, when you submit all of your decisions to Christ, your life will become much easier and more fulfilled. There is far less stress knowing that it was God's decision.

All of this sounds nice, but how do you actually go about submitting your decisions to Christ's will? Well, the process is similar to the steps you should take to remove an addiction from your life.

1. UNDERSTAND WHY IT'S IMPORTANT

My purpose in writing this book is to help Christians understand the importance of their identity. When you know how important it is to submit your decisions to the supreme decision-maker, you will take steps and adopt disciplines to act accordingly. In reading this book, can you agree with me how important it is to find identity in Christ?

2. PRAY CONTINUALLY

This could easily be number one, but it's also a continual way of life, so it's not entirely accurate to place it in sequential order at all. Just know that prayer is essential to finding identity in Christ. I suggest praying out loud rather than in silence. When I began praying out loud rather than in my head, I began to see huge transformations in my life and found more security in Him. Proverbs 18:21 puts it this way: "The tongue has the power of life and death." When you speak to the Lord, He speaks back!

3. COMMIT TO FOLLOWING HIS LEADING

You must decide that He is the leader of your life. Make it a conscious decision. Don't assume that just because you've been going to church and know a lot about the Bible that you have submitted all your life decisions to Him. Make this a conscious decision and tell yourself that you will follow God's leading in your life, no matter your physical circumstances or outcome. This is trusting His wisdom over your own. What is God asking you to do? Fast and pray? Quit your job? Move? Have a tough conversation that you've been avoiding? Commit to following His direction, no matter how uncomfortable!

4. CLEANSE YOURSELF

Think about any actions or behaviors you have that separate you from your identity in Christ or compromise your fellowship with Him. Bring those actions and behaviors to the light. Do you look at images you shouldn't? Do you use vulgar language? Are you easily angered or offended? Do you compare your life to someone else's? These behaviors are not aligned with your identity in Christ. When you are out of alignment, you are bound to make decisions that look very different from the ones you would make if your identity were submitted to Christ. Think about these sins consciously, then deliberately bring them to the surface. Now resolve that you will destroy them. You must destroy anything that comes into conflict with your identity in Christ. Until you do, you will continue to be prey to the anxiety that comes with internal conflict.

5. PRAYERFULLY BRING EVERYTHING TO GOD

Reflect on your actions throughout the day and determine if you have done something that is out of alignment with His direction. When you indulge in sin, you are acting in direct opposition to your identity in Christ. As you become more aware of the identities that lead you, you can begin to destroy the ones that lead you down the wrong paths.

Identity in Christ brings peace. There is no confusion is His direction. Furthermore, it brings comfort that He is in control. It may seem scary to give someone else control of your life, but the truth is you were never truly in control. The truly scary place to be is not knowing *who* is in control. If your identity is not found in Christ, it will be found in something else. And that means your actions are controlled by something else. If

I'm doing something I know displeases Christ, I'm not acting in my true identity in Him.

After reading this chapter, I encourage you to go through the five steps again. Ponder how these five steps can relate to your life and daily decisions. Use those five steps to make it a habit to consciously submit all your decisions to Christ every day. Remember, having multiple identities that compete for control of your life is a natural part of being human. And it's not abnormal in our walk with God to be led astray from time to time by an identity that has taken inappropriate priority. Remember: those identities the disciples struggled with were not bad; they were simply following a good identity at an inappropriate time.

One final word of assurance: as we grow in our awareness of the identities that vie for our attention in pressure situations that demand action, we can better assess the situation, make better decisions, and take more appropriate steps in response.

16

HUMILITY IS ABILITY

WHEN PRIDE COMES, THEN COMES DISGRACE, BUT
WITH HUMILITY COMES WISDOM.
PROVERBS 11:2

Nice guys finish last. I'm sure you've heard this phrase at some point in your life. The suggestion is you cannot get ahead in life if you're always nice to people. The flip side to this being if you're highly successful, you must not be a very nice person. Now, these things may be true at times on a surface level, but are they the rule? Does being a nice person keep you from getting ahead in life?

The simple answer is, it depends on which race you're running.

In this chapter, we'll take a closer look at humility. True humility is always – 100% of the time – a result of finding and becoming fully aware of your identity in Christ. Immediately, this challenges the world's view that humility is having a low value of yourself. Finding identity and value from Christ is the highest value you can have. Being a son or daughter of God is the top. There is nothing higher. But how can being at the top bring humility?

When I search for humility online, the first definition that comes up is: "a modest or low view of one's own importance." This couldn't be further from the truth. However, it does reveal how the world sees this topic. Sadly, this definition is forced on us by a world view that's completely out of alignment with our Christian faith, and it couldn't be more misguided. Furthermore, this definition is why we fight humility so much. Do you want to go through life having a low opinion of yourself? Neither do I.

The Merriam-Webster Dictionary does a little better defining humility but still misses the mark with: "freedom from pride or arrogance: the quality or state of being humble." But is that all it is? The lack of pride or arrogance? That seems to further the idea that humility detracts; that it signals the lack of a trait (pride or arrogance) rather than being a trait of its own.

In this chapter, I will challenge these two definitions because they both miss the truth about what it means to live in humility. If we are to live lives of heartfelt service, we must understand God's definition and embrace humility as a desirable trait in our walk with Christ. If the opposite of lack is abundance, then His definition will reveal how this one trait can endow us with a wellspring of abundance from which we serve others.

What are the downsides that come to mind when we think about humility? In our society, it carries the label of weakness. We think humility will take away our individuality. The world tells us that humble people get pushed around and bullied. The inherent message portrayed is you cannot reach success by being humble. The result is the fear of living a humble life.

According to the world, humility will keep you from having ambition, winning competitions, rising to meet a confrontation, or having any financial success. The world says humility will keep you in a low lifestyle. If we allow these worldly concepts to shape our thinking, we will bristle when God's word calls us to be humble. Many of us hold reservations because of the thought of what we might lose. After all, God certainly doesn't want us to be pushovers, right?

First, we need to see the fallacy in the phrase, "nice guys finish last." The assumption behind this statement is that being nice means you let people walk all over you. Conversely, it suggests that having boundaries is proof that you're not nice. It sounds ridiculous when I put it that way - but think about it. The suggestion that you cannot be intelligent, smart, and successful in the world without treating people like garbage along the way is ridiculous. However, if we're not careful, we may find ourselves, subscribing to that erroneous way of thinking. I challenge you to reject anything suggesting that being a good person is in any way a weakness or hindrance in your life.

Worldly thinking like this will not allow you to find your identity in Christ and fulfill the destiny He has in store for you. On the other hand, when you find your identity in Christ you will automatically challenge the rules of the world and test them against God's word.

Let's examine again the fallacies stated in the definitions I found online of humility. It calls humility a modest or low view of one's own importance. Then the Merriam-Webster Dictionary calls it the freedom from pride and arrogance. Now, if we combine those two definitions, we find the suggestion the world is trying to make. According to the combined definition, your importance or value is defined by your pride or arrogance. Now we're seeing how silly those definitions are. Humility is indeed on the opposite spectrum of pride, but to lack pride is not to lack importance or value. Being prideful has nothing to do with how you value yourself. Prideful people do not have a true vision of their value, which is why they try to assert their value – often through boastful arrogance. To put it another way, pride does not equal value or importance.

The reason pride seems so attached to humility is because someone who does not have a proper view of their value in Christ will likely chase after pride. Pride is actually a result of lacking humility. The worldly suggestion is that humility is an empty cup void of pride. Humility is not the opposite of pride in the way that is being suggested in the same way full and empty are opposites. Pride is a cup filled with artificial value. Humility is a cup filled even higher with *true* value and worth. Humility is reached when we know our value is higher than anything our earthly actions can achieve for us.

In this sense, pride and humility cannot coexist. However, a prideful person can have a mask of humility that fits the accepted definition.

I was once watching a dance competition where one of our studio teams was competing. After each team's performance, the host spoke to their leader on stage. Something one team leader said forever stuck in my head: "We pride ourselves in our humility." Wow! What a statement. I immediately turned to Claire and expressed the impossibility of such a state of being. However, I have learned to see things differently since then. As God has taken me on this journey to discover my identity in Christ, I have come to understand how this can happen. Let me explain how I think this can happen.

Priding ourselves in our humility means trying to be humble enough to be a better person. Furthermore, it is thinking we are better than others because we are humble. It is consciously making an effort to show others that we are humble and making it known. In Matthew 6:16 Jesus instructs against such false humility by saying, "When you fast, do not look somber as the hypocrites do, for they disfigure their faces to show others they are fasting." They were not doing this out of love for God; they were doing it for the benefit of being seen by other people. We must be very careful with public displays of humility.

The interesting thing about pride in humility is that such a person understands the value of being humble but they have a warped view – the worldly view – of what humility is. Pride in humility is finding identity in how others view you. Pride in humility is trying to become a better person through action rather than allowing humility to be a result of the true knowledge of your worth.

Humility is a state of awareness more than anything. Humble people derive their value from Christ and do not concern themselves with how others view them. True humility is living in full awareness of your individuality while also being aware that you have the exact same value as the person next to you. That is why a humble person does not allow their individuality to define them.

A humble person is not easily intimidated because they are aware of their value. This is where many people get the idea of humility wrong. Humility is not weakness. A humble person cannot be bullied because you cannot bully someone who has a clear identity. If you know fully within yourself that your value is identical to that of the next person, you will not succumb to someone else attempting to assert themselves as better or higher than you.

One day while I was in the Marines, as I was pulling into my barracks parking lot I happened to be talking on the phone while driving – which is not allowed. A few fellow Marines from another unit saw me and confronted me in a very aggressive and inappropriate manner. One of them was literally in my face yelling at me.

What did I do? Nothing.

After the incident, I told my superiors what happened and they came out and we all went and had a talk with them. When I spoke further about it with my peers, embarrassment made me try to rationalize my lack of action. *Well, I didn't think it was a good idea to be fighting in the barracks parking lot, right? I mean, I don't want to get in trouble with the chain of command after all.* My friends acknowledged my reasoning, probably just wanting to make me feel better. However, the truth was I was being bullied and I was acting – or not taking action – out of fear.

Being intimidated or fearful is not a display of humility. This is the second type of false humility. The person who rationalizes their fear by claiming they were being humble has the wrong view of humility. If someone screams in my face and I do nothing about it, one of two things has happened. Either I was afraid to do something, or I had full power to do something and decided to do nothing because that was the right course of action. Although the outcome may be the same, the factors involved in the decision are very different.

True humility is awareness *and* power.

You've likely heard someone say something like, "I wanted to slap them, but I took the high road." Perhaps they did make the decision out of humility, but the need to explain their inaction suggests otherwise. The need to save face is an indication that they find their value in how others view them. True humility does not seek validation from others.

Keep this in mind when you encounter such situations; you can be humbled without having humility. In other words, you can be bullied, belittled, embarrassed, and forced into servitude without having a humble spirit. Again, humility is a state of mind.

Obviously, I'm not suggesting humility will cause you to get into physical confrontations. Far from it. My point here is that there's a difference between inaction motivated by fear and choosing not to act out of humility because it's the right thing to do. Humility is an awareness that the attacker's current actions and my response do not determine my value.

These are the two big false humilities: pride in humility and fear of acting.

It is easy to get caught up in the worldly definition of humility. The world would have us thinking humility is simply submitting to others all the time and having a low self-worth. Humility is viewed as a weakness by Western society. Although we claim it to be a good trait, we don't usually encourage it in those we care about. The reason for this conflict is our warped view of what it means to be humble.

The Bible instructs us to be humble over 70 times, so it must be a good trait. However, being weak and having low self-worth are certainly not traits to strive after.

Thus, if we believe the Bible only has good instruction for our lives, we know humility is not weakness. Jesus was far from a weak man and He was the embodiment of true humility. Therefore, we must conclude that the humility the Bible talks about is far different from the world's definition.

It is clear that the humility the Bible refers to is not the same humility referred to by the world. Biblical humility is the awareness of who you are and who everyone else is. The world tells us to determine everyone's value by their titles and accomplishments. Identity in Christ says we are to value everyone the same way God does; everyone is worthy of the blood of Jesus. Humility comes from a true understanding of who you are and who others are, regardless of surface portrayals.

When you are fully aware of who you are and the value Christ has placed on you, you cannot allow someone to treat you poorly. Therefore, it is not humility to stay in a toxic environment. It is not humility to keep allowing someone to speak negatively into your life. Again, humility is awareness and power!

I'm going to tell you a truth that may be difficult to hear – but please receive it in love. Allowing someone in your life to assume a higher value than you is *idolatry*, not humility.

Jesus already determined your value on the cross. On the flip side, thinking of yourself as higher in value than others is idolatry as well because Jesus also determined their value on the cross. We are not all the same, but we are all equally worthy of the blood of Christ. We don't have the same roles in life, we don't make the same amount of money, drive the same cars, live in the same neighborhoods, or have the same life experiences, but we do have the same Savior and the same price tag. 1 Corinthians 6:20 says, "you were bought at a price." That price was the highest price possible.

Now, with the appropriate awareness of what humility is, you can live free from condemnation and judgment. Not freedom from the judgment of others, but also freedom from condemning others. Humility does not allow you to find your value or the value of others in anything other than being a child of God. Humility does not need the affirmation or approval of others. There is nothing wrong with validation, affirming words, kind interactions, and building one another up. These are all good things. But they are not where your true worth comes from.

Humility sees beyond your ability to be well-spoken, have a following, or become successful in your field.

So what can we conclude about the difference between the Bible's definition of humility as opposed to the world's? I want to drive home the alternate paradigm that we receive from the Lord: one that is in opposition to the normal definition of humility.

There is no lack in humility. Humility is ability. Humility is not having a low self-worth; it is having the highest self-worth possible. Humility is the awareness that everyone has the same value.

Humility is the ability to gain power, knowledge, wisdom, money, titles, or even fame without finding your value in those things. Humility is the ability to be in the presence of someone of great worldly stature and having the full awareness that your value is *identical* to theirs. Humility is the ability to have fun in competition without finding your value in who wins.

Humility is one of the highest manifestations of our identity in Christ.

17

FOR THE SPIRIT GOD GAVE US DOES NOT MAKE US TIMID.
2 TIMOTHY 1:7

In this verse, we find Paul imploring his mentee not to be timid. If you've been in Christian circles for very long, you've probably heard Timothy identified as timid. This is where that belief originates. Paul wanted Timothy to realize his true identity in Christ and not be afraid of speaking out. However, I only gave you the first part of the verse. You see, the Bible is filled with verses telling you what *not* to do and who you are *not*. However, our God is not a God of lack. Here's the rest of the verse: "but [the Spirit] gives us *power, love, and self-discipline.*" [emphasis added]. Every time you see a verse of instruction concerning who you are *not*, it is almost always followed by who you *are*.

This is a crucial aspect to understand. Your 'I am' will always be stronger than your 'I am not' statements.

Again, when the Bible tells you who you are *not*, it then tells you who you *are*. If you want to grow into the fullness of who you are called to be, you must remove the negative identities that cause bad habits in our lives. This process starts with knowing who we *are* more than being aware of who we are *not*.

Knowing who you are is power.

Focusing on who you are not is loss.

Don't live a life of loss! Speaking power into your life is an important step in overcoming the negative identities that try to plague you.

Most of us have identified areas in our lives where we can improve and bad habits we want to remove. However, focusing on what we want to remove will decrease our chances of lasting change. This is where the popular self-help teaching has it right: start by finding your why. You need to know *why* you want to change. You need a reason for the goals you want to achieve. In the same way, goals of change are not usually big enough to motivate someone; the simple desire to remove something from our lives is not usually enough motivation to do it.

Knowing something is bad for you is not enough to keep you from doing it. If it were, you wouldn't be eating chocolate and scrolling through your phone for hours. You must combat the bad habit with a good identity that counteracts it. This is not the same as applying the 'chew some gum when you feel like smoking' idea when your goal is to stop smoking. This is about identifying one of your strong values that is contrary to the habit you want to remove. For example, if you don't want your children to see you smoking, you can successfully combat your smoking habit by focusing on your identity as a good parent, which is in direct conflict with your desire to smoke. I've never smoked, so I'm speaking a little out of my element here, but hopefully, you understand the meaning.

Let's revisit the nature of a couple of habits I've mentioned in previous chapters. When I was single, I gambled at the casino often. I had racked up quite a bit of debt as a result of my irresponsible gambling. After I got married, I continued this bad habit in the beginning. But then something happened that made me realize I needed to stop.

You remember the story. I lost $300. That was a lot of money for me at that time. Afterward, I called my wife, Claire, and told her about it. This experience caused me to realize something. Something clicked in my head that said, "You're married now, you have responsibilities, and you need to take care of your money." I didn't make the decision not to gamble anymore, but I did decide to act as a responsible husband and man who is smart with money. When I gave that identity a high priority in my hierarchy of identities, I was compelled to stop gambling because gambling does not fit in with being responsible with money.

Another addiction I had to overcome was pornography. I was able to beat this addiction similarly: by attaching a higher priority to my role within the family and focusing on what a godly husband and father was supposed to look like.

Upon meeting with my accountability partner in the battle against pornography, he shared a very powerful Bible passage with me that is very relevant to this topic. After hearing these verses, the dynamic of having an overriding identity made more sense. Maybe it will help you contextualize it in your mind as well. In Matthew, Jesus tells us what happens when we try to remove an impurity from our lives and leave an empty, clean house afterward.

WHEN AN IMPURE SPIRIT COMES OUT OF A PERSON, IT GOES THROUGH ARID PLACES, SEEKING REST AND DOES NOT FIND IT. THEN IT SAYS, 'I WILL RETURN TO THE HOUSE I LEFT.' WHEN IT ARRIVES, IT FINDS THE HOUSE UNOCCUPIED, SWEPT CLEAN, AND PUT IN ORDER. THEN IT GOES AND TAKES WITH IT SEVEN OTHER SPIRITS MORE WICKED THAN ITSELF, AND THEY GO IN AND LIVE THERE. AND THE FINAL CONDITION OF THAT PERSON IS WORSE THAN THE FIRST.
-MATTHEW 12:42-45

The key phrase I want you to notice here is "unoccupied, swept clean, and put in order." This person was free from some impurity after cleansing their body and mind of this evil. However, they did not have anything in there to replace it. When the evil spirit returned, he found his old house unoccupied. The scariest part of this parable comes at the end: the final state of that person was at least seven times worse than the first! This is a strong warning against removing things from your life without a clear purpose and reason for doing so. You must combat bad habits by prioritizing positive identities that demand positive, life-affirming action.

As Christians, we have Christ living in us. However, we often hold onto unoccupied spaces in our lives even after conversion. These are secret compartments in our hearts that we've reserved for bad habits. The misconception is that when we remove something from our lives, we are cleaning and clearing out our lives. This is not the method Jesus was advocating in Mathew. Jesus wants us to drive out the impurities by filling our lives with the Holy Spirit. This is not a lack. When the Spirit fills us, there is no opportunity for lack or unused/wasted space.

It may seem counterintuitive, but when you focus on what you want to remove, you are focusing on an area where you want to see empty space – lack. The very act of focusing on that area opens the door for impure thoughts and habits to rush in.

Conversely, when you focus on the positive things you want to see in your life — a positive identity — you open the door for that identity to be strengthened in your nature as one who has been reborn.

Think about the Israelites who were destined to take possession of the Promised Land. The Lord commanded them to drive out the occupying tribes before taking up residence there. Taking up residence is the key phrase here. The Israelites did not drive out the previous occupants and then leave the land empty. The Israelites occupied the land themselves! Therefore, the Promised Land was never empty. The Promised Land can be an allegory of our destiny in Christ to live a pure life. It would have been silly for the Israelites to leave that great land empty, right? So why do we think we should simply drive bad habits out of our life without occupying that space?

God has promised us freedom, power, and a sound mind! Allow His Spirit to fill your entire heart!

This realization can transform the way you look at your life and the way you pray to God. Sometimes we get caught up asking—even begging—God to remove impurities from our lives. This is fine, but removing them is not enough; we have to replace impurities with the fullness of the Holy Spirit.

Let me be clear. I'm not speaking about removing a bad habit and replacing it with a better habit. I'm proposing that you start by recognizing that the habit is not who you are in Christ. Then remove that habit by pinpointing an identity in your life that the bad habit cannot coexist with, and focus on making that identity a priority.

All of your bad habits are in contradiction to your identity in Christ. However, a general knowledge that you are a child of God is not usually enough to remove them from your life.

I know it doesn't sound very Christian-like to say that, but follow me for a minute.

The reason I came to this conclusion is this: how many people claiming to be Christians continue to sin in ways they know is wrong? The understated answer is a lot. Sometimes they even use their knowledge of Scripture to justify their sins. You know, the 'grace, not works' argument. This is why I say a general knowledge of your true identity is not enough to combat these sinful habits. You need to be in touch with specific positive identities that are aligned with your identity in Christ. That doesn't mean you won't still have conflicts, but it does mean that as you focus on your positive identities, gradually, everything you do will begin to fall in line with His direction for your life.

Let's do a little exercise. You may want to get a pen and paper for this section.

Take the time to figure out what your negative identities are. Think of things you've thought of yourself, have been spoken over you, or you feel other people impose on you for whatever reason. First, add 'I am not' to them and then counter them with two or three 'I am' statements that empower you to abandon those negative identities. If you do this exercise, don't get lazy and simply counter it with 'I am not.' That's a detracting identity, anchored in lack. You must refuse to identify with what you are not. I encourage you to write these down and ponder the truth.

Here are some examples:

I am not timid – *I am* a child of God who has a valid opinion. *I am* courageous and have a responsibility to openly stand for truth. *I am* a father who wants my children to have a good example and know the difference between right and wrong.

I am not worthless – *I am* valuable. *I am* immensely valuable because Jesus died for me. My worth is found in the price Jesus paid for me.

I am not an angry person – *I am* a respectful person who knows the value of others is identical to mine. *I am* a child of God with full knowledge that others are also children of God. *I am* responsible for my emotions; others cannot control them.

I do not lust – *I am* a child of God who recognizes lust is not His way for me. *I am* a husband who loves his wife and has promised to be faithful. *I am* a father with daughters watching me and watching the way I look at other women.

You see, we can go on and on with this. Did you catch the identities and the short definitions?

Also, note the similarities of the 'I am' statements I call upon to battle impurities in my life. The good news is that even one strong positive identity will battle multiple negative traits. Therefore, the strongest identities in your life are often the ones you will call upon to bring you out of various bad behaviors. You're not seeking a new identity; you're seeking to live up to and strengthen something that you already are—something that is already at work in you.

Everything must fall in line. Here's an example of an identity hierarchy: I am a child of God. I am a servant. I am a good husband. I am a good father. I am a provider. I am a protector. I am financially responsible. I am healthy.

Now out of those eight identities, at least two of them will directly counter bad habits and sinful areas of my life. Yes, I have more identities below those, and those lower identities must fall in line with the ones above. These identities help me make decisions and govern my actions. Notice there are no 'I am not' statements in my identity hierarchy. 'I am not' statements have no place in your hierarchy either because any 'I am not' statement can be correctly countered with a positive 'I am' statement. Identities anchored in 'I am' leave no room for a void or empty spiritual space.

The reasons mentioned above should clarify why it is more important to focus on who you are rather than who you are not. It is easier to overwhelm bad with good than to remove bad without making a replacement. I read once that Mona Lisa refused to profess negative sentiments or to join 'anti' movements aimed at injustice because she was not 'anti' anything, she was 'pro' the opposite. When we focus on removing, we come from a place of lack. When we focus on the positive, we come from a position of strength and empowerment.

Having the Holy Spirit in your life does not constrain you to a life of lack. Everything He wants for you is good. If you find yourself looking at the negative things in your life – things that you want to remove – I encourage you to repeat the 'I am' exercise I outlined above. Write down each habit you want to remove and counter it with a powerful 'I am' statement that cannot coexist with the bad habit.

Too often we, as Christians, focus on what we cannot do. The heart is right, but the focus is wrong. Jesus has not condemned you to a life of shame and boredom because you can't do all the fun stuff your friends are doing. He is inviting you into a life of freedom and fulfillment.

The problem comes when Christians mistake freedom to mean "do whatever you want." However, the freedom Christ gives is the freedom from slavery to sin. Freedom to live in the calling He has provided. He does not ask us to start picking away at who we are by taking out all these bad things. Rather, He reveals to us who we really are and empowers us to conform to that image by getting these things out of the way.

We are not digging out and cleaning a glass filled with dirt and leaving it sparkling clean and empty; we're filling up a glass with truth and finally using that glass for its intended purpose.

Make no mistake about it: those filthy habits and sins cannot coexist with your identity in Christ. And take heart: your position in Christ is the most free and amazing place to live!

18

DO NOT JUDGE, AND YOU WILL NOT BE JUDGED. DO NOT CONDEMN,
AND YOU WILL NOT BE CONDEMNED. FORGIVE, AND YOU WILL BE FORGIVEN.
LUKE 6:37

Throughout this book, we dived into various identities and the meaning of finding identity in Christ. Although the focus has been much on you, it's time to take the next step and level up on your identity. The principles shared in this chapter are the true litmus test of your identity in Christ.

It is impossible to live in your identity in Christ if you cannot view others through the lens of *their* identity in Christ. Why? Because you cannot understand your own value if you undervalue others. If you think a homeless person has less value than you, then you have missed what it means to be a child of God.

Furthermore, undervaluing others leads to a legalistic view of our worth. If I think I'm more valuable than the man asking for money on the street corner, I believe my status and accomplishments in life determine my value. Now, how can I possibly take that same view and stand next to the President of the United States and claim that my value is equal to his? I can't. The way I assess value cannot be determined by anything on this earth, because value is inherited from God. He paid the same price for us all, so our value is identical.

When I see someone whose lifestyle is of lesser quality than my own (based on a worldly standard) I have a choice as to how I will act and treat that person. I can put them down, degrade them, or have a general disrespect for their position in life. Regardless of their situation or status, the way we view others speaks volumes about how we see ourselves. The reason I refer to this world view as legalistic is because it values people based on their works and achievements. If we assess our worth in terms of something achieved or gained, we will always be able to find someone else who is worth more.

Each time you encounter another person, you have a choice. You can see that person for who they appear to be on the outside, or you can see them for who Christ says they are. Jesus paid the same price for us all. So to view them as Christ views them is the simplest solution because there is only one value for all. However, I admit it is not easy to live in this state of mind.

When we see a homeless man, we may look at his situation and value him based on the way he values himself. After all, he doesn't appear to value himself very much, so why should we value him? Didn't he chose that lifestyle and so chose to devalue himself? I'm not responsible for his value, right?

While it is true that I am not responsible for the homeless man's value, it is also true that his value does not differ from mine. Whether or not *he* understands his value does not determine his *true* worth. His *perception* of his worth is not reality and should not be the image that you and I choose to see.

You may be thinking this is not something you struggle with – and maybe it is not. However, I think this type of devaluation of others creeps up in our lives more often than you may realize.

How about lust? Have you ever heard someone attempt to justify their objectification of someone based on the way she dressed or how she presented herself? You've probably been living under a rock if you haven't heard a phrase like, "Well, she's asking for it by dressing that way." This is not a gender-biased phrase, by the way. I've heard it from women and men alike. Men use this as an attempt to justify their lustful indulgence, and women use it as a means of judgmental condemnation.

Now, let me back up here for a minute. Am I saying that the statement is not true? No, the statement itself may be true, but what you do with that truth determines whether or not it is a heart issue. You must understand that the objective truth of a statement should not determine how you treat others.

When a man lusts after a woman, he is reducing her from a human being with a soul down to an object. Yes, women can lust as well, but I will stick to speaking about men because, as a man, I refer to these principles from that perspective. It is impossible to see a woman as a child of God while viewing her as an object in your fantasy.

Let me use an illustration: if a woman comes into your line of sight and you see a lot of skin, you have a choice. Your choice determines who you turn the power over to.

If you choose to indulge your fleshly desire and take the opportunity to keep looking and take in every curve and shape, you are refusing to take responsibility for your actions. If you think you are powerless to resist the urge to turn her into an object in your mind, then you are handing power over to your flesh.

If you use the excuse that it's because she is dressed that way, you're handing over the power of your morality to *another person.* That is simply saying her choice of clothing determines whether you will value her – and others like her. Indeed, she may not value herself outside of her appearance. However, if you allow the way she values herself to determine the way you see her, you have fully missed an opportunity to see her as a child of God.

Again, this goes back to the way we view ourselves. Lust is devaluing someone in your mind based on their outward appearance. If I cannot view others as equal in value to myself, I cannot view myself as equal in value to others who appear to be of higher status in the world. If all it takes to strip away my view of value – which was determined by God – Is for a scantily-clad woman to come into my line of sight, I am not living in the true value system designed by my Creator. My value system would then be situational and determined by the people with whom I interact.

On the other hand, if I catch a glimpse of the woman coming into my line of sight and avert my eyes or otherwise choose not to indulge my fleshly lust for her, I'm mentally making a statement of how I assess her value. In other words, I will not allow her fleshly portrayal of her self-worth to determine the way I view her or treat her. If I struggle with this type of thing, it is best to honor my convictions by looking away.

Now, I know how this may sound contradictory, but let me clear this up. You may be thinking that the fact that I turned away when she came into my line of sight proves that I'm still being controlled by her choice. Not necessarily. I chose to look away because I choose to value her according to God's standards. Adopting that line of thinking is what controls my choice. To indulge in lustful pleasure is to opportunistically reduce others and undervalue them based on the way they choose to present themselves. On the other hand, to look away is to honor her value as a daughter of God who deserves dignity and respect, whether or not she appears to respect herself. Therefore, I'm choosing to protect my identity and value in Christ by looking away.

Here's a great tip I learned from Dr. Doug Weiss: An excellent approach to take in this particular arena is to pray for her. When you consciously pray for that woman who expresses a low sense of her own value, you honor her as a daughter of the Most High God in your mind. Remember, this is about the view you choose to adopt, not the way she views herself.

I want to be very clear about something. There is a larger principle at work here, one which extends beyond the issue of men and their lust. I offer this illustration because it is the easiest way I can think of to highlight the root problem. The root problem is that we tend to value others based on the external factors they present to the world. When you allow other people's choices and views of themselves to determine the way you value them, you do not see them as children of God.

Furthermore, it reflects the way you value yourself. If you cannot look at her clothing, job, tattoos, appearance, or lifestyle without assigning her value based on those things, you cannot see your own true worth as determined by Christ's blood.

We are called to view others as valuable because God considered them valuable enough to send His Son to die for them. Imagine you are standing before God, and He asks you how you treated His sons and daughters, your brothers and sisters: how well did you love them, care for them, and respect them? Now imagine this is your answer: "Well, Lord, I think I did pretty good. I loved everyone as much as they loved themselves. I cared for them if they took care of themselves. And I respected them if they respected themselves." Although this seems a preposterous answer, it is easy to fall into this line of thinking. However, when I put it that way, I'm sure you see the problem. Furthermore, if you're anything like me, you've fallen into this legalistic world-view many times.

This is where we need to draw the line as true followers of Christ who understand our true worth. We have a responsibility to value ourselves and those around us as children of God. We are not responsible for how *they* view themselves but that should not affect how *we* see their value. If we take a moment to relate this idea to the previous chapter about humility, we realize that having a complete and authentic view of our worth and the worth of others allows us to live within our true worth and treat others accordingly.

Consider the following equations that illustrate how the world assigns value.

Poor person < middle class.

CEO > employees.

You see the pattern. The list goes on. We are constantly told to base others' value on their status as perceived by the world. Furthermore, this problem is not exclusive to "the world." This type of value system exists in the church as well. Think about it this way.

Pastor > deacons.

Elders > church members.

Christians > atheists.

Again, this list could go on for days. If your value is based on external factors, including those choices made by the person in question, you are not maintaining a value system put in place by God.

If your value system reflects a focus on titles, social status, education, etc., you will constantly be looking for ways to exalt yourself above others or determine your standing in a crowd.

What does the Bible have to say about this subject? Let's take a look at 2 Corinthians 5:14-16.

FOR CHRIST'S LOVE COMPELS US, BECAUSE WE ARE CONVINCED THAT ONE DIED FOR ALL, AND THEREFORE ALL DIED. AND HE DIED FOR ALL, THAT THOSE WHO LIVE SHOULD NO LONGER LIVE FOR THEMSELVES BUT FOR HIM WHO DIED FOR THEM AND WAS RAISED AGAIN. SO FROM NOW ON WE REGARD NO ONE FROM A WORLDLY POINT OF VIEW. THOUGH WE ONCE REGARDED CHRIST IN THIS WAY, WE DO SO NO LONGER.

These are some powerful statements about who we are, how much Christ values us, and how we should value others.

Allow me to paraphrase this verse and add some commentary. It is because of Christ's love that we are compelled to love others because of our assurance that He died for everyone. This is based on our assurance of how much He valued everyone, regardless of their concept of their own self-worth. Our estimation of others' value is not determined by how they value themselves. He died for everyone so that we could look to Him for a true assessment of our worth, rather than looking to the world and our status to determine our value.

This is followed by the clearest statement yet—one that needs no paraphrase or commentary. It summarizes everything I've addressed in this entire chapter so far: *"So from now on, we regard no one from a worldly point of view."* Whereas we may have adopted this point of view at one time, we no longer hold that view. We now value others based on His sacrifice for us on the cross.

You are responsible. God has entrusted you with the responsibility of valuing others. You do not have any control over *other people's* responsibilities—only your own. You are not responsible for the way others view themselves, but you *are* responsible for how *you* view them. As you adopt the proper view of others, you will gain a proper view of yourself.

It is impossible to view yourself as equal in value to others if you have a diminished value of anyone else. Think about the truth of that statement. This is not an abstract thought; it is a fact!

If we are all of equal value in God's eyes, then you cannot be more valuable than anyone else.

Therefore, to consider yourself as more or less valuable is not a godly view of true worth. Identity in Christ and humility demand a vision of true worth determined by the blood of Jesus. Having a true understanding of our worth in Christ coincides with having the full awareness of everyone else's *identical value.*

Every person in the world has experienced hurts and pain throughout life on Earth. People have various coping mechanisms and ways to medicate their pain. The external things we see are often simply manifestations of those pains and hurts that we cannot see. If we translate the outer manifestation of their pain into a low estimation of their worth, then we are taking advantage of that pain and acting like a bully and a predator. You are not a predator; God has called you to be a protector.

You are a son or daughter of God who fully understands your true value and the value of others as equal to your own. The Holy Spirit has given you insight, understanding, and the power to see the world through God's eyes. Use that awareness to protect others from your own lustful desire for worldly power as determined by worldly values. The world tells you to take advantage of weakness and assert dominance in all situations. In so doing, it urges you to compare yourself to others and maintain your focus on competing with them. But an awareness of your true worth says God determined your value as equal to theirs from the beginning, so there is never a need to compete for artificial value.

The underlying theme in this chapter is to recognize where your responsibility lies. You are not responsible for the value they place on themselves, but you are responsible for how you value them. You are not responsible for their pain and hurt, but you are responsible for the way you respond to it. You are not responsible for how they treat themselves, but you are responsible for how you treat them. Unless you can esteem others with the highest value regardless of their situation, you cannot live in your own true identity in Christ.

True worth is found when you can see others as having a value identical to your own.

19

WHAT DOES GOD SAY ABOUT YOU?

"FOR I KNOW THE PLANS I HAVE FOR YOU," DECLARES THE LORD, "PLANS TO PROSPER YOU AND NOT TO HARM YOU, PLANS TO GIVE YOU HOPE AND A FUTURE."
JEREMIAH 29:11

So what does God have to say about all this? Once you know the effects your identities have on your life, it is useless if you don't use that knowledge to live in your true identity, which is determined by God.

I want to emphasize the importance of knowing God's word is for *you*. As Christians, I think we often listen to sermons and scriptures without personalizing the message to ourselves. When I realized that Jesus loved me – not just the whole world – it changed my perspective. I started to realize that He actually does care about what I do, my pains, my struggles, and my life. When you can take scripture and apply it directly to your life you make that word so much more powerful.

So what does God have to say about who *YOU* are?

The best way to find out what your identity is as God intended it to be is to look in Scripture. When you know who you are in Christ and who God intended you to be, your daily decisions become easier, the way you treat others improves, and your peace of mind skyrockets. You will find as God takes you deeper into discovering your identity in Him, your emotional fitness will improve, and you will feel less tossed and turned by the various circumstances in your life. Identity in Him and the knowledge that you belong completely to God is the most freeing place to be as you go through life.

Again, to find your true identity in Christ, you must know what He says about you. In this chapter, I will layout some Scriptures about our true identity and offer some commentary on them. I hope that these will be firmly planted in your being and remind you of who you are. I also hope you will allow them to truly manifest themselves in your decisions and actions every day.

The following are beautiful verses that give hope in who you are. However, I believe most people reading or preaching on these verses focus only on the "I am" statement. Too often, they skip the fact that almost every verse that proclaims your identity in Him also comes with instruction on what that identity means. Therefore, with each verse, I will also expound on the expectation He places on you based on who He says you are. That's right, God has expectations of you as His beloved child. With each verse, I will give commentary on who God says you are, what it means, the expectations that come with who you are, and an 'I am' statement *just for you*. I encourage you to repeat the 'I am' statements to yourself out loud. So let's get started!

THEN GOD SAID, "LET US MAKE HUMAN BEINGS IN OUR IMAGE, TO BE LIKE US. THEY WILL REIGN OVER THE FISH IN THE SEA, THE BIRDS IN THE SKY, THE LIVESTOCK, ALL THE WILD ANIMALS ON EARTH, AND THE SMALL ANIMALS THAT SCURRY ALONG THE GROUND."
GENESIS 1:26 NLT

Who you are

To understand His true intention for your life, let's go to the beginning. First of all, you were made in His image. This is the unique trait humans have over every other creature on Earth. Nothing else was created in His likeness. This was our original calling as humans. Therefore, this is a special honor bestowed on us.

What it means

You were created to reign and rule over every other type of creature on Earth. Nothing else on Earth was given the mind of Christ and called to rule. Therefore, this is a special privilege based on who God says you are. This brings with it the responsibility of care and concern for all other life on Earth.

Your 'I am' statement

I am made in His image, and I am responsible for the care of all the creatures on Earth.

FOR WE ARE GOD'S MASTERPIECE. HE HAS CREATED US ANEW IN CHRIST JESUS, SO WE CAN DO THE GOOD THINGS HE PLANNED FOR US LONG AGO.
EPHESIANS 2:10 NLT

Who you are

You are a masterpiece created by the master artist. This verse truly speaks to your value in Him. Other translations use the word 'workmanship.' This is one of my favorite verses that speaks about who we are in Christ. I am amazed to think the Creator of the universe took time to create me anew as His masterpiece. A masterpiece is no simple work of art; it is something that the artist took time on, put a lot of thought and effort into, and something He is proud of. You are His masterpiece!

What it means

He has made you into a new creation so you can do the good things He planned for you. First of all, let's look at the fact that He has a plan for you. Long ago, Jesus had a plan for your life. This is a comforting thought. Furthermore, as His masterpiece, you are expected to do those good things.

Notice the order of the Scripture. We were created as new creations upon acceptance of Jesus; therefore, we do good things. It is not the other way around. Doing good works does not make you a child of God, but as a His child, you certainly are expected to do good works. It's important to keep these in proper order.

Your 'I am' statement

I am a masterpiece designed by God Himself. He has big plans for my life. That is why I do good things.

SO WE ARE CHRIST'S AMBASSADORS; GOD IS MAKING HIS APPEAL THROUGH US. WE SPEAK FOR CHRIST WHEN WE PLEAD, "COME BACK TO GOD!"
2 CORINTHIANS 5:20

Who you are

You are an ambassador of Christ! That's exciting. This means He has called you to serve His purposes and appointed you with focused intentionality. He has a specific message to present to the world through you. To be an ambassador means the entity who placed you in that position trusts you to speak on their behalf. The person who appointed you as ambassador believes you understand and can portray their message in a way that represents them. Furthermore, they have given you the authority and anointing to deliver that message. This is no small assignment.

What it means

When you serve as an ambassador for someone else, you have been entrusted with great power and responsibility. I'll say it again; this is no small assignment that God has placed on you. You are a physical representation of His words. As an ambassador, you cannot speak words that fail to reflect the thoughts and intentions of the entity for whom you represent. This speaks to the importance of close fellowship with Him. If you do not nurture constant communication and fellowship with Christ, you cannot stay in tune with all He wants you to say and do in any given situation. Furthermore, as an ambassador, you are to reflect the person of Jesus. Others are meant to see Him in your actions and hear His words when you speak. Think about the weight of this assignment. This removes any notion that it is acceptable to speak idle words or have momentary slip-ups. Does it happen? Sure. However, it will happen less if you truly live in your identity in Christ: the one that affirms that you are His appointed representative to the world.

Your 'I am' statement

I am an ambassador of Christ Jesus. As I live out the specific mission he has assigned to me, my actions and words reflect His actions and His words.

Side Note:(This awareness of your identity as an ambassador of Christ should be enough to stop most bad habits if you truly believe this statement about yourself.)

In this next commentary, I will combine three verses.

BUT TO ALL WHO BELIEVED HIM AND ACCEPTED HIM, HE GAVE THE RIGHT TO BECOME CHILDREN OF GOD.
JOHN 1:12 NLT

FOR YOU ARE ALL CHILDREN OF GOD THROUGH FAITH IN CHRIST JESUS. AND ALL WHO HAVE BEEN UNITED WITH CHRIST IN BAPTISM HAVE PUT ON CHRIST, LIKE PUTTING ON NEW CLOTHES.
GALATIANS 3:26-27 NLT

FOR HIS SPIRIT JOINS WITH OUR SPIRIT TO AFFIRM THAT WE ARE GOD'S CHILDREN. AND SINCE WE ARE HIS CHILDREN, WE ARE HIS HEIRS. IN FACT, TOGETHER WITH CHRIST, WE ARE HEIRS OF GOD'S GLORY. BUT IF WE ARE TO SHARE HIS GLORY, WE MUST ALSO SHARE HIS SUFFERING.
ROMANS 8:16-17 NLT

Who you are

You are a child of God and an heir to His inheritance. This is a very comforting statement. When you accepted Jesus into your life, you became a son or daughter of the Most High God. Heirs do not earn their way into their inheritance; it is given by birthright.

What it means

As a child of God, you can walk in the confidence that you belong to Him. Your value and worth have already been determined as well as your inheritance. Let me expound with an earthly relationship example. My children do not need to figure out daily whether or not they belong to me; there is no question. Their identity as children of mine is not called into question when they do something wrong. However, as a father, I do place expectations on them. Because they love me as their father, they will want to do good things that please me. On the other hand, if they choose not to meet my expectations, it will impact their experience as my children, but it could never change my love for them or the fact that they are my children. Knowing your value as a child of God and having the confidence that your birthright cannot be taken from you is a complete gamechanger.

Your 'I am' statement

I am a child of God. My value and worth have already been established by the One who created me and adopted me as His child.

DON'T YOU REALIZE THAT YOUR BODY IS THE TEMPLE OF THE HOLY SPIRIT, WHO LIVES IN YOU AND WAS GIVEN TO YOU BY GOD? YOU DO NOT BELONG TO YOURSELF, FOR GOD BOUGHT YOU WITH A HIGH PRICE. SO YOU MUST HONOR GOD WITH YOUR BODY.
1 CORINTHIANS 6:19-20 NLT

Who you are

You were bought at a high price by the blood of Jesus on the cross. Therefore, you no longer belong to yourself; you belong to Him. Furthermore, your body is a temple in which God reigns. This is a very high-value identity statement. You are so valuable to God that He allowed His Son to be brutally killed so that *you* could be saved. What a high price to pay! As I have explained in previous chapters, your value cannot get any higher. Your worth cannot be contained in any definition the world can conceive, any title you can attain, or any achievement you can accomplish. Your value is set by the price Jesus paid for you.

What it means

To have been bought at a price means He paid for you. Therefore, you and I belong to Him. These verses tell you to honor Him with your body. You (and me) are to live free from the lustful and selfish desires of the flesh and conduct yourself in a manner that is pleasing to the One who made you, Jesus Christ.

Your 'I am' statement
I am worth the highest price possible, and Jesus paid that price for me. As a temple of God, I honor Him with my body.

AND, 'HE IS THE STONE THAT MAKES PEOPLE STUMBLE, THE ROCK THAT MAKES THEM FALL.' THEY STUMBLE BECAUSE THEY DO NOT OBEY GOD'S WORD, AND SO THEY MEET THE FATE THAT WAS PLANNED FOR THEM. BUT YOU ARE NOT LIKE THAT, FOR YOU ARE A CHOSEN PEOPLE. YOU ARE ROYAL PRIESTS, A HOLY NATION, GOD'S VERY OWN POSSESSION. AS A RESULT, YOU CAN SHOW OTHERS THE GOODNESS OF GOD, FOR HE CALLED YOU OUT OF THE DARKNESS INTO HIS WONDERFUL LIGHT.
1 PETER 2:8-9 NLT

Who you are
These verses are filled with descriptive words that express what God has done for you and how He sees you. He has called you out of the darkness into His wonderful light. As Christ-followers, we are His chosen people, royal priests, a holy nation, and God's very own possession. I love how Peter takes the time to give us multiple descriptive titles that define who we are. This tells me Peter understood the importance of title identities and how people can relate so easily to them.

What it means
Once again, you see the expectations attached to the titles God ascribes to you: expectations and responsibilities concerning actions you are to take. (*Did you ever meet a priest or pastor who didn't have responsibilities?*) You must be careful not to overlook the full import of

these verses. In saying that you are to come out of the darkness and show others the goodness of God, Peter elaborates by pointing out that this is a call to come out of hiding, to be bold, and to claim, proclaim, and project your identity as a child of God – one belonging to Him. This verse implores you to live into your true identity as ascribed by God and not hide amid the darkness of the world.

Your 'I am' statement
I am chosen by God to be a royal priest for Him, so I will proclaim His name and boldly live my life for Him in the light.

BUT YOU HAVE AN ANOINTING FROM THE HOLY ONE, AND
ALL OF YOU KNOW THE TRUTH.
1 JOHN 2:20

Who you are
You are anointed by God. This statement often recurs in the Bible. We hear it so often that we must be careful not to overlook it. It carries so much meaning! You have an anointing from the Most High God, you know the truth, and God truly has a plan for *your* life and a calling specific to *you.*

This next section may elicit some questions in your mind. As you're reading it, I implore you to re-read the scripture and see for yourself if it agrees with what I state in the following.

What it means
When we receive Christ into our lives, we often ask the question, "Now what?" We might start by asking Christians who seem more spiritual than we are, asking if we need to change certain behaviors. Or we might seek the leadership of a pastor as to how we are

supposed to live now. This verse tells me we are often seeking answers we *already* know. When you have Jesus in your life, the knowledge of His direction for your life has already been imparted to you. *You know the truth!* Whether you decide to live your life according to that truth or not reveals where you find your true worth and identity. If you know your value as determined by God, you will follow His leading in your life. *I'm not saying you shouldn't seek godly counsel or ask questions of those who have been walking with Jesus longer than you have.* However, you should not base who you are on what someone else tells you; rather, you should base it on what *God* tells you.

Your 'I am statement'
I am anointed by God Himself, and I know what is right; therefore, my actions are directed by Him.

STAND FAST THEREFORE IN THE LIBERTY WHEREWITH CHRIST HATH MADE US FREE, AND BE NOT ENTANGLED AGAIN WITH THE YOKE OF BONDAGE.
GALATIANS 5:1 KJV

Who you are
You have been set free by Christ's sacrifice on the cross! Jesus came down and died so that you can experience true freedom in Him. This verse is a call to claim your freedom in Him and protect it with a tight grip.

What it means
To experience freedom in Christ means you are no longer bound to sin and rules. Therefore, once you have experienced that freedom, you are exhorted never to turn back to the things that once bound you. You should never again be tangled in the yoke of bondage. You have escaped – or have the freedom to escape – the

bonds that enslaved you to your addictions, bad behaviors, and bad habits. You must cling to your new identity and stand firm in the freedom He has given *YOU*.

Your 'I am' statement

I am free in Christ; therefore, I will never again turn back to my old ways.

I hope you have basked and absorbed what these verses proclaim and describe about who you are in Christ. The Bible is filled with identity statements and examples that ascribe high titles to you, place expectations on you, and give responsibilities to you. When we know who we truly are in Christ and the high price He paid for us, we can understand our true worth and live in accordance with these titles assigned by God.

Note: Not one of these descriptive identities in the Bible is something you can achieve or attain through your own accomplishments. There is nothing you can do in your own power to conform to or earn these descriptions. However, once you receive identity in Him, you are empowered to fulfill the expectations attached to each Biblical description. Your identity in Christ allows you to make decisions, take actions, and treat people as He designed, according to who you are in Him. Your worth and value is defined by God; therefore, you no longer need to derive your value from the way others view you. Your value has already been determined on the cross.

20

A NEW CREATION

I HAVE BEEN CRUCIFIED WITH CHRIST AND I NO LONGER LIVE, BUT CHRIST LIVES
IN ME. THE LIFE I NOW LIVE IN THE BODY, I LIVE BY FAITH IN THE SON OF GOD,
WHO LOVED ME AND GAVE HIMSELF FOR ME.
GALATIANS 2:20

Throughout this book, we've gone down many paths and explored various areas of who we are and what motivates us to act as we do. Perhaps this was a simple journey of knowledge for you. On the other hand, these principles may have taken you on a roller coaster of emotion and self-realization. Either way, I hope that as you read through these pages, you came to a greater awareness of your value as determined by God. Defining your value by His standards is the only way to truly live into His plan and His design for your lives.

When I felt God urging me to write this book, I did not know exactly who my audience would be. However, as I immersed myself in the project, He revealed messages along the way and poured the words out onto these pages through me. I slowly realized this was for people who are just like me. Although I was raised in a Christian home with loving parents, I did not fully come into the realization of my value as a child of God until a few years ago. I tried many things to find my identity during my adult years – and they all came up short.

At some point, I realized that those worldly pursuits reflected confidence issues that had dogged me my whole life.

I routinely attempted to hide those issues and compensate for them by attaining titles, achievements, and new skills and abilities. In the process, I've attained various titles and achievements; Marine, husband, high wage earner, business owner, and father. However, even after adding each one of those achievements, what I found within myself never changed. I was still the same self-conscious person. The reason I couldn't establish a strong identity in those things—one that filled me with confidence—was because they were artificial. On an intellectual level, I already knew that. Those artificial identities didn't change the fact that my heart screamed for meaning. That is where my identity in Christ finally came in and altered my perspective in life-changing ways. Nothing could fill that God-shaped hole inside my heart except Him. When that realization led to a new paradigm for my life, everything changed. So no matter what your walk and your journey of self-discovery looks like, I hope this book has helped you build your awareness of these issues.

Addressing such a broad subject within the pages of a single book has been a challenge, but the message is simple. Your true worth is determined by Jesus' blood on the cross, and nothing else can be of a higher value than that sacrifice.

The beautiful thing about identity in Christ is that it allows for our individuality to be defined by other identities unique to us. We don't have to abandon titles, achievements, education, and other things that have given us artificial value when we come to recognize our true worth. Rather, they are enhanced by our central identity in Christ—as long as they are properly prioritized in the hierarchy. When the light of the Holy Spirit fills our life, it is impossible not to shine in every area of our lives – as long as each of these identities has been consecrated to Him.

If we have a warped view of identity we will likely continue in behaviors and choices that conflict with our identity in Christ. However, our growth in the knowledge of who we are in Him will cause us to abandon such vices.

The realization of who we are in Christ brings clarity of mind, peace in our hearts, and security in our interactions. When you are fully attuned to your value as defined by Christ, and you have established this as your firm foundation, you no longer attach importance to other people's opinions of you. When a coworker talks behind your back, or someone else takes credit for something you did, or you catch the blame for something over which you had no control, those things will no longer have the power to steal your peace. Why? Because your value is not found in them.

Furthermore, finding identity in Christ is always accompanied by humility. Humility will give you a proper perspective of your true worth. Not only will you value yourself, but you will also value others in new ways. The flawed worldly view of humility says if you are humble you value others as greater than yourself; however, that is far from the truth. True humility gives you an awareness of the true worth of every person, yourself included.

God assigns the same value to everyone. We have each been bought with the blood of our Savior Jesus Christ, an event that determined our worth years ago. It is impossible to have a value greater than the sacrifice He made for us when He paid for our salvation with His life.

That value - determined by God – is valid across the board. The way we view others and the value we assign to them reflects the extent to which we value ourselves. We cannot have a proper view of our worth if we do not value others in equal measure.

Your worth was defined by the ultimate sacrifice He made before you were born. When Jesus died on the cross, He paid the highest price possible for you. In economics, we learn that the value of any item or service is defined by the price someone is willing to pay for it. You can set the price of milk at $10, but if nobody will pay that price, then the milk is not worth $10. In the same way, the high price Jesus was willing to pay for us has determined our value—not what we think or what others think about our status, achievements, skills, titles, or education. This is the true worth assigned to you by the highest authority. There is only one man who had the means to pay such a high price for you, and He paid that price at the cross.

I hope this book and these words have had as much impact on your life as they have had on mine. I challenge you to enter the paradigm I have presented in these pages when thinking of who you are and assessing your own value. Bask in the glory and knowledge of what it means to be a child of God. Live into the fullness of His plans for your life. Live a life free of what others think. Make your decisions based on His direction. Stand fast in the liberty in which Christ has made you free, and never allow yourself to be held in the bondage of false identities again.

THANK YOU FOR READING THIS BOOK!

I would love to hear from you!
I really appreciate all of your feedback, and I love hearing what you have to say.
I need your input to make the next version of this book and my future books better.
Please leave me a helpful review on Amazon letting me know what you thought of the book.
   Thank you so much!
   -Michael J. Lewis

CONNECT WITH MICHAEL:
WWW.TRUEWORTHMEDIA.COM/CONTACT-US
E-MAIL: TRUEWORTHMEDIA@GMAIL.COM
FACEBOOK: WWW.FACEBOOK.COM/TRUEWORTHMEDIA

Michael Lewis has a heart to see the church revived and uplifted through expository teaching, raw Gospel truth, and logical thinking. It is his mission in the church to see men and women have tough conversations and disagreements without bickering and fostering bitterness. He sincerely believes this can be attained by focusing on The Way, The Truth, and The Life. Identity in Christ will set us free from the bondage of bitterness and posturing for position.

Michael resides in Colorado Springs with his wife, Claire, and his three daughters.

Claire is the author of *The Star in You.*

FOR MORE INFORMATION, VISIT WWW.TRUEWORTHMEDIA.COM

Made in the USA
Columbia, SC
01 October 2020

21830623R00124